About CHARA
Josephso

We all need help in developing ~~........~~ __ ᵼ just happen, nor is it easy. But the benefits are iɴᴄaɪᴄuɪable. Young people especially need guidance and example — from parents, always, but also from schools, businesses, and other community institutions acting in concert. In a pluralistic society, effective character education rests on the enduring values that we all share, regardless of cultural, political, religious and economic differences.

These are the operating beliefs of a nationwide, grassroots education initiative called CHARACTER COUNTS!. A diverse alliance of thousands of schools, government agencies, nonprofit groups and businesses work together as the CHARACTER COUNTS! Coalition to reinforce millions of young lives with core ethical values called the "Six Pillars of Character": trustworthiness, respect, responsibility, fairness, caring and citizenship. To draw attention to their year-round character-education efforts and results, communities across the country celebrate the third week of October as CHARACTER COUNTS! Week.

CHARACTER COUNTS! — as well as the *Pursuing Victory With Honor* sportsmanship campaign, the *Honor Above All* academic integrity campaign, and the *Foundations for Life* essay contest — are projects of the Josephson Institute of Ethics, a teaching, training and consulting organization. The Institute encourages people to make principled decisions and carefully consider the effects of their choices. Since 1987 it has provided services and programs for thousands of leaders — in government and the armed forces, in business and media, in law and law enforcement, and in education and the nonprofit community. Former law professor and businessman Michael Josephson founded the Institute in honor of his parents and serves as its president on a volunteer basis. A volunteer board of governors oversees the Institute, a 501(c)(3) nonprofit corporation funded by revenue from programs, products and publications as well as by gifts and grants.

To help individuals improve, the Institute seeks to:
- Stimulate moral ambition.
- Heighten the ability to perceive the ethical dimension of choices.
- Teach how to discern the most effective ethical responses.
- Show how to implement these responses intelligently.

The Institute seeks to enhance organizational ethics by inspiring leaders to:
- Identify the ethical obligations arising from positions of authority.
- Consider the impact of all institutional actions on all stakeholders.
- Create workplaces that reward ethical and discourage unethical conduct.

The Institute's services include:

- Presentations and keynote addresses
- Workshops, seminars and community forums
- Customized on-site training
- Ethics audits and consulting
- Standards/codes of conduct
- Media commentary
- Character Development Seminars
- *Pursuing Victory With Honor* sportsmanship seminars
- *Honor Above All* academic integrity campaign
- *Foundations for Life* quotation-based essay contest
- Ethics and Effectiveness in the Workplace seminars
- Publications, videos and communications

For more information about CHARACTER COUNTS! and the Josephson Institute:
9841 Airport Blvd., #300
Los Angeles, CA 90045
(310) 846-4800
(800) 711-2670
www.charactercounts.org
www.josephsoninstitute.org
www.FFL-essays.org

"Teachers affect all eternity. You never know where their influence stops."
— Henry Adams

"Inviting our students to take the pursuit of happiness seriously means accompanying and challenging them along the road to virtue."
— John Adams

Copyright © 2005 Josephson Institute of Ethics

Distributing Publisher
Unlimited Publishing LLC
Bloomington Indiana
www.unlimitedpublishing.com

Contributing Publisher
Josephson Institute of Ethics
Los Angeles, California
www.josephsoninstitute.org

UNLIMITED
PUBLISHING

JOSEPH & EDNA
JOSEPHSON
INSTITUTE
OF ETHICS

Cover Design: Peter Chen

First Edition

Copies of this fine book and many others are available to order at:
www.charactercounts.org and
www.unlimitedpublishing.com/authors

ISBN 1-58832-133-9

Unlimited Publishing
Bloomington, Indiana

Josephson Institute of Ethics
Los Angeles, California

What Every Educator and Youth Leader Must Know:

The Case for Character Education and CHARACTER COUNTS!

By

Mark Britzman
South Dakota State University

Wes Hanson
Josephson Institute of Ethics

Michael Josephson, founder and president of **CHARACTER COUNTS!**, developed many of the concepts and ideas this book addresses.

A production of the Department of Publications and Communications at the Josephson Institute of Ethics

Wes Hanson	Steve Nish
VP/ Department Director	Senior Editor / Webmaster

Dan McNeill	Melissa Mertz	Andrew Acalinovich	Peter Chen
Editor	Instructional Designer	Art Director	Assistant Editor / Graphics

Unlimited Publishing
Bloomington, Indiana

Josephson Institute of Ethics
Los Angeles, California

Table of Contents

Introduction 1

Why Character Education Matters 2

What We're Up Against 5

How We Got Here: A History of Character Education in America ... 14

The Advent of **CHARACTER COUNTS!** 25

The **CHARACTER COUNTS!** Approach 34

Principles of Effective Character Education 46

A Closer Look at the Six Pillars of Character 59

Putting It All Together: Making Good Decisions 77

Conclusion: Leaving a Legacy of Change 87

Introduction

What does it mean to educate young people? What do they need to learn? Academic skills are obviously important — but it is not enough to be smart or knowledgeable, to be able to pass a test. As a glance at the headlines will attest, too many "successful" people lack character, and their wavering moral compass needles lead them into disappointment and scandal.

Written for you, this book explains character education in depth. Character education is hardly new. Societies have practiced it since ancient Sumer. It only fell out of favor in the 20th century, but has steadily gained adherents over the last two decades as citizens have realized the frightening and depressing consequences of its absence, and resolved to act.

This book tells you why character education matters, what happened to us without it, and how you can bring it to your schools.

In particular, this book introduces you to an approach to character education that has rapidly become the nation's most widely implemented, by far. It's called **CHARACTER COUNTS!**, and through 4,200 schools and leading social service agencies it promotes universal, nonpartisan values called the Six Pillars of Character: trustworthiness, respect, responsibility, fairness, caring and good citizenship.

CHARACTER COUNTS! has grown so rapidly because it delivers results. It drastically cuts misbehavior and delinquency, and improves students' commitment to school. It frees teachers to do what they want to do — teach, and build the future. It is not an "add-on" to further burden educators and youth leaders, but rather works pervasively. A nonprofit, national coordinating office supports it with an array of top-flight, highly regarded training services, programs and materials.

We hope this volume inspires you to institute character education as you seek to create and sustain the most effective learning environment. No job is more important than yours.

– w.h.

Why Character Education Matters

Here's a true story about the power just one teacher has to make a difference.

Michael Josephson — founder of the Josephson Institute of Ethics and its **CHARACTER COUNTS!** youth-education project — interviewed a panel of high school students in Illinois, all of whom had been in trouble more than once. He asked them whether anyone at the school had really influenced their ideas about right and wrong.

He heard about Ms. Hubbard, a woman who was passionate and vocal about what she wanted for these youngsters. She took every opportunity to challenge and lecture students about good decisions and safe living. She was well known for her "mantra" — "no sex, no drugs, no violence" — which she would shout while patrolling the halls and yell out into the parking lot from classroom windows.

"Preaching is a pretty primitive form of teaching," Mr. Josephson remembers, "so I asked whether it worked. To my surprise, every student said it did."

Jose said, "It just burns a hole in your head. No matter where you are you think about what she says: no sex, no drugs, no violence."

"It makes you feel guilty," said one.

"You don't want to let her down," others added.

Another student, LeVesta, said, "You know when she sees you on Monday she's going to ask you what you did."

Mr. Josephson asked, "Why do you care about what Ms. Hubbard says or thinks about you?"

In different words they all came up with the same answer: "Because she cares about us." Some of these kids don't get much caring at home. LeVesta, who got straight F's before Ms. Hubbard took an interest, said, "She made me think that I mattered and that I could have a future. And I believe her. Now I get B's and want to go to college."

When Mr. Josephson asked Ms. Hubbard how it felt to hear about her impact, she began to weep. She had no idea, she said, that she was so important to these kids, no idea how much respect they had for her and how much her caring meant to them.

Ms. Hubbard motivated her students because she demonstrably cared about them. She reinforced her admonitions by asking the kids on Monday morning what they had done over the weekend. She made LeVesta and others want to be better because they became convinced they had a future.

Our Children's Future, Our Own

We all want today's youngsters to thrive and be productive citizens. We must ask, "How do we want our youth to act when they reach adulthood and how do our educational efforts serve that end?"

Life is much more than standardized tests, though academic achievement is obviously important. But employers are also interested in hiring individuals of character who are dependable and work well together.

Pursuing our own interests (including knowledge and grades) comes naturally. But we must also make decisions that are ethical, taking into account the interests of others and the long-term implications of our choices.

Such decision-making prowess does not come naturally. We have to carefully model, teach and nurture it — in the home primarily, but also in the arenas of education, community life and workplace. Dealing every day with our most impressionable citizens, the school is in a unique position to influence what our society will be.

To understand the fundamental importance of character, ask yourself some questions: Would you rather be married to someone you trust or not? Would you rather your co-workers or neighbors respected you or not? Would you prefer your children to be responsible or undependable? Do you want a society of justice? Would you like to fly on an airplane whose pilots cheated on their training exams, or lie in a hospital where the doctors had fudged their way through medical school?

Obviously, we all would like others to have good character. But remember: the best place to start is with ourselves, which always remains the greatest challenge.

What We're Up Against

"There is a hole in the moral ozone," Michael Josephson says, "and it's getting bigger."

Josephson Institute studies show that large numbers of young people grow up without a commitment to the ethical values needed to energize the conscience and guide behavior. "As a result," Mr. Josephson says, "they lack internal mechanisms to help them know right from wrong and to generate the will power to exercise self-control and consistently do what is right. Increasing proportions of youth from all over the country, from advantaged as well as disadvantaged backgrounds, are demonstrating wanton disregard for fundamental standards of ethical conduct."

The most recent Josephson Institute Report Card on the Ethics of American Youth, conducted in 2004, found glaring discrepancies between students' admissions of unethical acts and their self-assessments.

According to the national survey of 24,763 high school students, nearly two-thirds (62 percent) cheated on exams and more than one in four (27 percent) stole from a store within the past 12 months. Additionally, 40 percent said they "sometimes lie to save money."

Despite these admissions, 74 percent rated their own ethics higher than those of their peers and almost all (98 percent) said it was important for them to be a person of good character. What's more, most had unrealistically high self-images when it comes to ethics. Here is one survey question: "If people you know were asked to list the most ethical people they know, how many would put you on their lists?" Eighty-three percent said at least half the people they knew would list them. Additionally, 92 percent said they were satisfied with their ethics and character.

The inconsistency may arise from impressions about the larger world around them. High levels of cynicism about the ethics of successful people and the prevalence of cheating in the "real world" may create an apparent justification for dishonest conduct. Cynicism is especially strong in young males. Two-thirds indicated a belief that "in the real world, successful people do what they have to do to win, even if others consider it cheating" — and more than half (52 percent) the females concurred. In addition, half (51 percent) of the males agreed with: "A person has to lie or cheat sometimes in order to succeed." About one-third (32 percent) of the female students expressed a similar view.

When asked to prioritize their values, most high schoolers expressed commitment to positive views. Thus, 91 percent said it is very important to have "trusting personal relationships," 87 percent said it is very important to "treat others with respect," and 84 percent said it is very important to have "good moral character."

Analyzing the survey results, Michael Josephson said, "Though the Report Card on the Ethics of American Youth continues to contain failing grades, there is reason for hope. For the first time in 12 years the cheating and theft rates have actually dipped downward and the stated devotion to ethics is the strongest we've seen. While this results in a troubling inconsistency between words and actions, character education efforts should be able to build on the fundamental appreciation of ethics, character and trust to achieve continuing improvements in conduct. Still, it can't be comforting to know that the majority of the next generation of police officers, politicians, accountants, lawyers, doctors, nuclear inspectors and journalists are entering the work force as unrepentant cheaters."

The survey gauged student ethics in 85 schools throughout nation (45 percent public schools, 40 percent private religious schools and 15 percent private nonreligious schools). Roughly the same number of males and females answered the questions. Here are the results in detail:

Attitudes About Ethics, Character and Trust

Young people were almost unanimous in saying that ethics and character are important on both a personal level and in business, but they expressed very cynical attitudes about whether a person can be ethical and succeed.

- **Importance of Character and Trust.** Virtually all high school students (98 percent) agreed with the statement: "It's important for me to be a person with good character."

  — 98 percent believe that "honesty and trust are essential in personal relationships."

  — 97 percent said, "It's important to me that people trust me."

  — 84 percent said, "It's not worth it to lie or cheat because it hurts your character."

- **Ethics in the Workplace.** Highly publicized business scandals have undoubtedly influenced their cynical attitudes about real-world ethics, yet young people still believe ethics is important in the workplace. Ninety-four percent said that "in business and the workplace, trust and honesty are essential."

- **Goodness More Important Than Wealth.** Ninety percent agree that "being a good person is more important than being rich" (though 15 percent of males *disagree* compared to only 5 percent of females).

- **Role Models.** Despite a growing concern that young people lack positive role models, 84 percent say that "most adults in my life consistently set a good example of ethics and character."

  — Though one justification for the rampant cheating is the pressure parents put on youngsters, the overwhelming majority (91 percent) say that their parents or guardians "always want me to do the right thing, no matter the cost."

  — Only 6 percent say that their parents "would rather they cheat than get bad grades."

- **Playing by the Rules.** The vast majority rejected cynical statements about the propriety of cheating to win.

  — Only 13 percent agreed that "it's not cheating if everyone is doing it."

— Only 8 percent agreed that "in sports, if you are not cheating, you're not trying hard enough."

— Only 8 percent *disagreed* with the statement: "People should play by the rules even if they lose."

- **Self-Appraisal.** Despite admissions of high levels of lying, cheating and theft, the students think very well of their character and ethics, both in relative and absolute terms.

    — 92 percent said they are "satisfied with my own ethics and character."

    — 83 percent expected that half or more of all the people who knew them would list them as one of the most ethical people they know.

    — 74 percent said, "When it comes to doing what is right, I am better than most people I know."

What Motivates Young People?

When asked to rate the importance of values including wealth, looks and popularity, the vast majority of adolescents ranked virtuous qualities and behavior above materialistic and pragmatic ones.

- 91 percent said it is very important to have ***trusting personal relationships***.

- 87 percent said it is very important to ***treat others with respect***.

- 84 percent said it is very important to have ***good moral character***.

- 73 percent said it is very important to ***help others***.

- 70 percent said it is very important to be ***thought of as ethical and honorable***.

- 63 percent said that *religion* is very important to their lives, but fewer (55 percent) said it is very important that they *live up to the standards of their religion*.

- 54 percent said it is very important to be *charitable*.

Though it is not clear that their conduct jibes with their stated priorities, with the exception of *getting into college* (which 87 percent rated as very important), only a minority of high school students said that non-character attributes were very important.

- 42 percent said it is very important to be *physically attractive*.

- 28 percent said it is very important to be *wealthy*.

- 19 percent said it is very important to be *popular*.

- 16 percent said it is very important to be *famous*.

Cynicism

Despite consistently expressing positive attitudes about the importance of ethics and the role their parents and teachers play in encouraging them to do the right thing, a very high proportion of young people reveal cynical attitudes about what works and doesn't in the real world.

- 59 percent agreed that "in the real world, successful people do what they have to do to win, even if others consider it cheating" (66 percent males, 52 percent females).

- 42 percent believe that "a person has to lie or cheat sometimes in order to succeed" (51 percent males, 32 percent females).

- More than one in five (22 percent) believe that "people who are willing to lie, cheat or break the rules are more likely to succeed than people who do not."

Conduct

Deep and widespread youth cynicism often shows itself in rationalizations that nullify ethical judgment and attempt to justify conduct that is contrary to stated moral convictions. Thus, the same youngsters who speak of the importance of ethics, character and trust frequently lie, cheat and even steal without much guilt or hesitation.

The good news is that while students continue to lie, cheat and steal at alarming rates, it appears that the tide has shifted, and for the first time in 12 years of surveys, scores in each category actually improved. We have no solid explanation for this turnaround, though we know that the spread of character education programs and the new attention to values after 9/11 and the staggering corporate frauds at firms like Enron may have had an effect.

It is also possible that, with all the publicity on cheating, students may be less honest on surveys than before. In fact, the admitted cheating rate may understate actual behavior, as 29 percent admitted they lied on one or two questions on the survey (12 percent said they lied on three or more).

In any event, the amount of confessed dishonesty demonstrates that schools have a very long way to go to better instill attitudes and habits of integrity.

- 82 percent admitted they *lied to a parent* within the past 12 months *about something significant* — and 57 percent said they lied two or more times. In 2002, 93 percent said they lied to parents.

- 62 percent admitted they *lied to a teacher* within the past 12 months *about something significant* — and 35 percent said they lied two or more times. In 2002, 83 percent said they lied to teachers.

- 35 percent *copied an Internet document* within the past 12 months — and 18 percent did so two or more times. This question was not asked in 2002.

- 62 percent *cheated on a test at school* within the past 12 months — and 38 percent did so two or more times. In 2002, 74 percent admitted cheating on an exam.

- 83 percent *copied another's homework* within the past 12 months — and 64 percent did so two or more times. This question was not asked in 2002.

- 22 percent *stole something from a parent or relative* within the past 12 months — and 11 percent did so two or more times. In 2002, 28 percent admitted stealing from a parent or relative.

- 18 percent *stole something from a friend* within the past 12 months — and 7 percent did so two or more times. In 2002, 22 percent admitted stealing from a friend.

- 27 percent *stole something from a store* within the past 12 months — and 13 percent did so two or more times. This is a huge drop from 2002 when 38 percent admitted stealing from a store.

- 23 percent *cheated or bent the rules to win in sports* within the past 12 months — and 12 percent did so two or more times. This question was not asked in 2002.

Violence and Disruptive Behavior

Violence is an especially serious breach of morality, and both it and its risk factors demand thorough scrutiny. The figures below, from several sources, show the scope of the problem.

Evidence of Bad Choices. The evidence is overwhelming that our youth are making more bad choices than ever before and are not just another generation "carrying on." For instance, violent and disruptive behavior is becoming frighteningly common in our public schools and class-rooms. Teachers said in 1996 — for the first time — that disciplinary problems were the main reason they left the profession (Langdon, 1996). According to the same poll, the public said that "lack of discipline" and "fighting, violence and gangs" were the "biggest problem[s]" facing local schools.

Police Intervention. In a 1997 study of secondary school principals, 50 percent of them required police intervention at least monthly for violent acts occurring in their schools, and 52 percent said that they were facing serious gang problems (National Association of Secondary School Principals, 1997).

Weapons and Violence. The Josephson Institute's national youth survey in 2004 found that 10 percent of high school students said they'd taken a weapon to school at least once in the past year. Fifty-four percent of all high schoolers said they'd hit a person within the last 12 months because they were angry. Broken down by sex, 62 percent of high school males and 46 percent of high school females had struck someone for this reason. Furthermore, 42 percent of all high school males and 17 percent of females felt it was sometimes OK to hit or threaten a person who made them angry.

Threats and Attacks. According to a study from the Research Triangle Institute, 25 percent of eighth and ninth grade students have witnessed threats to teachers, while 37 percent of eighth and ninth grade students feared attacks at school (Silvia, Thorne & Tashjian, 1997). In the National Center for Education Statistics survey "Violence and Discipline Problems in U.S. Public Schools: 1996-97," 10 percent of all public schools experienced one or more serious violent crimes (murder, rape or other sexual battery, suicide, physical attack or fight with a weapon, or robbery) during the 1996-97 school year and reported it to law enforcement. Forty-five percent of elementary schools reported one or more violent incidents, compared with 74 percent of middle and 77 percent of high schools during 1996-97 (Heaviside, Rowand, Williams & Farris, 1998).

Feeling Unsafe at School. It's no wonder then that the Josephson survey (2004) found that 20 percent of all high school students do not feel very safe at school. Males are more likely to feel unsafe than females (21 percent vs. 19 percent).

Breakdown of Respect and Courtesy. In the classroom, there is a breakdown of respect and common courtesy. The percentage of elementary teachers who say students disrupt the classroom most of the time or fairly often has increased from 48 percent in 1984 to 65 percent in 1997. The percentage of elementary school teachers who say students talk back and disobey teachers most of the time or fairly often has increased from 42 percent in 1984 to 54 percent in 1997 (Langdon, 1997). Seventy percent of all high school students say "unruly students" distract them and undermine classes (Johnson & Farkas, 1997). Add to this problem the fact that 19 percent of high school males say they have been drunk at school at least once in the past year (Josephson Institute of Ethics, 2004).

Notes

1. Langdon, C.A. (1996). The third Phi Delta Kappa poll of teachers' attitudes toward the public schools. *Phi Delta Kappan, 78.*

2. National Association of Secondary School Principals (1997). *Safety issues serious in nation's schools: Principals taking action.*

3. Silvia, S., Thorne, J., & Tashjian, C. (1997). *School-based drug prevention programs: A longitudinal study in selected school districts.* Research Triangle Park, NC: Research Triangle Institute.

4. Heaviside, S., Rowand, C., Williams, C., & Farris, E. (1998). *Violence and discipline problems in U.S. public schools: 1996-97.* U.S. Department of Education, National Center for Education Statistics. Washington, DC: 1998.

5. Langdon, C.A. (1997). The fourth Phi Delta Kappa poll of teachers' attitudes toward public schools. *Phi Delta Kappan, 79, 3.*

6. Johnson, J., & Farkas, S. (1997). *Getting by: What American teenagers really think about their schools.* New York: Public Agenda.

How We Got Here: A History of Character Education in America

Character education, once the norm, fell into discredit with the advent of well-intentioned but ultimately misguided educational theories. It has enjoyed growing popularity over the last decade, but educators should be mindful of the events and ideas that led to its downfall, so they can better understand the overall moral environment and the challenges they face. This knowledge can also strengthen your resolve and bolster your arguments if you are challenged about the importance of character education.

Education: Historical and Worldwide Advocate for Ethical Living

All major civilizations have taught youngsters about ethical living. The world's great philosophical thinkers — from Socrates to Dewey, from Confucius to Buddha — have advocated living according to principle, not expediency. Religious and secular education have both traditionally emphasized both mind and morals. As education scholar Thomas Lickona (1992, p. 6) has written, "Down through history, in countries all over the world, education had two great goals: to help young people become smart and to help them become good."

Character Education in America. The founders of the United States asserted that moral education was essential for the success of a democratic society. "Their reasoning went like this," writes Lickona. "Democracy is government by the people; the people themselves are responsible for ensuring a free and just society. That means the people must, at least in some minimal sense, be good. They must understand and be committed to the moral foundations of democracy: respect for the rights of individuals, regard for law, voluntary participation in public life, and concern for the common good. Loyalty to these democratic virtues, Thomas Jefferson argued, must be instilled at an early age" (Lickona, 1992, p. 6).

Schools in the early days tackled the issue of character head on. Through consistent discipline, expectations for appropriate teacher behavior, and the curriculum, schools advocated the virtues of patriotism, hard work, honesty, thrift, altruism and courage (Lickona, 1992). "The leaders of the common school movement were mainly citizens who were prominent in their communities — businessmen, ministers, local civic and government officials. These people saw the schools as upholders of standards of individual morality and small incubators of civic and personal virtue; the founders of public schools had faith that public education could teach good moral and civic character from a common ground of American values" (Bennett, 1992, p. 58).

From the Bible to the "Natural Virtues." In the early days of the Republic, the Bible was the source book of both moral and religious instruction. As immigration increased and the nation became more diverse, character education grew less reliant on explicit biblical teaching. By the start of the 20th century, as the nation became a "melting pot" of cultures, various ethnicities and religions began to challenge the propriety of promoting Judeo-Christian ethics and beliefs. While many schools still taught the Bible, they also used the *McGuffey Reader* (a primary text to teach reading, heavily laced with ethical messages) and penmanship lessons (copying maxims about wisdom and virtue) to teach the "natural virtues" such as honesty, hard work, thrift, kindness, patriotism and courage. Character education through instruction, stories, example and discipline remained a central part of the educational mission.

Decline of Explicit Character Education and the Emergence of Three Philosophical Theories. The reasons for the decline in character education and public ethical instruction in the 20th century are complex and numerous, but three philosophical trends began undermining character education in the first half of the century.

- **Logical Positivism.** This theory discounted all value judgments and asserted that there was no valid basis for character education since there are no provable moral truths or objective standards of right and wrong.

- **Moral Relativism.** This theory held that moral values are simply a creation of culture, so universal ethical standards can't exist.

- **Personalism.** This theory held that each person should be free to choose his or her own values.

Other Factors in the Decline of Character Education

Contributing factors in the last 40 years most likely included a shrinking access to social connections, the impact of academic psychology, the ethical Sargasso Sea of "values clarification," increased stress on the family structure, the growing influence of mass media, and an overall decrease in religious involvement.

Shrinking Access to Social Capital. Robert Putnam, author of *Bowling Alone* (2000), believes that we became increasingly disconnected from family, friends, neighbors and social structures in the last third of the 20th century. "Social capital" is the reward of communal activity and community sharing, and our shrinking access to it is a serious threat to our civic, personal and moral lives. The perception of trustworthiness in a community encourages social and civic life. Social isolation, on the other hand, tends to breed moral decay. For instance, the following table shows the declining perceptions of honesty and morality in the last 50 years. When asked, "Do you think people in general today lead as good lives — honest and moral — as they used to?" Americans responded as follows:

Year	Those Answering "Yes"
1952	50 percent
1965	43 percent
1976	31 percent
1998	27 percent

(Putnam, 2000)

Putnam attributes the decrease in social capital to:

- Pressures of time and money, including the special pressures on two-career families

- Suburbanization, commuting and sprawl

- The effect of electronic entertainment — above all, television — in privatizing our leisure time

- Most important, generational change — the slow, steady and ineluctable replacement of the long civic generation by their less involved children and grandchildren (p. 283)

The Impact of Academic Psychology. Personality and character were once deemed interconnected. R. W. Gough (1998) believes that academic psychology has contributed significantly to the de-emphasis of character. He states, "Since the 1930s, in its efforts to become an objective science, academic psychology has almost exclusively talked in terms of personality, realizing that the time-honored notion of character was a richly ethical concept that couldn't be scientifically measured. Psychologists began defining 'the self' more narrowly in terms of personality 'traits,' such as assertiveness, self-esteem and compulsiveness, and thereby eliminated from their research the more holistic conception of human beings defined in terms of habits of character, such as honesty, respect and loyalty" (p. 6).

The Rise of Values Clarification, and More. To enhance self-esteem, teachers frequently encouraged students to clarify which values were important to them, without reflecting on how their values and resulting behavior affected others. "Values clarification is concerned not with which values people develop but how they develop their values. The approach seeks to promote growth, freedom, and ethical maturity" (Brooks & Goble, 1997). Values clarification can be very useful to determine a ranking of pragmatic or preference values. However, ethical values must be intact in the first place. Unfortunately, values clarification too often made the mistake of treating youngsters as if they already had a solid moral foundation. Hence, they merely had to clarify their values, and their ethical decision making would significantly improve (Lickona, 1992).

Values clarification helps individuals identify their actual values so they can feel better about what they do. It is rigorously nonjudgmental, meaning that it makes no distinctions based on the content of one's values. What a person wants and likes (personal preference values) and what she thinks will work (pragmatic values) are on an equal plane with beliefs about right and wrong (ethical values). As a result, values clarification tends to promote a highly ego-centered "whatever works for me" attitude towards values, which emphasizes consistency but ignores content.

According to Bill Honig (1986), "There's something absolutely essential missing from values clarification, and that's values, as the word is generally understood. While pretending to Olympian detachment in its neutrality on moral issues, values clarification actually affirms the shallowest kind of ethical relativism. It tells students that on matters of profound moral significance, their opinion – no matter how ill-informed, far-fetched or speciously reasoned – is all that counts. Ethics and morals are reduced to matters of personal taste. The issues of abortion and registering for the draft are weighed on the same personal, idiosyncratic scale as one's choice of spring clothing or vacation destination: It is so if you say it's so."

In addition to values clarification, other approaches to ethics became popular as replacements for character education or to justify its absence:

- **Ethical Relativism.** A form of moral agnosticism, this holds there are no standards of ethics, morality or good character. It therefore precludes moral judgment and reduces every ethical question to a matter of personal preference.

- **Indiscriminate Nonjudgmentalism.** Going a step further, indiscriminate nonjudgmentalism teaches that the only wrong is judging others ethically.

Ethical relativism and, to a lesser extent, indiscriminate nonjudgmentalism, base their approach to ethics on the many different social and cultural standards and traditions around the world. They point to these diverse and often contradictory beliefs and claim that no society has any greater claim to ethical wisdom than any other. Ethical relativism concludes all ethics are a matter of taste. Indiscriminate nonjudgmentalism concludes we have no right to judge the ethics of others.

These approaches have two great flaws: they cannot identify the moral difference between Adolf Hitler and Mother Teresa and they assume that cultures are inviolate (if the culture says it's moral, it's moral). For example, among the Tatar people in the Russian Republic of Tatarstan, the culture says, "If a man doesn't beat his wife, he doesn't love her." Is that moral? In the United States at one time, racial discrimination against people of color was a part of the national culture. But was it moral? Ethical relativism and indiscriminate nonjudgmentalism must answer yes or plead inability to answer.

While moral judgments should be made carefully and in a way that respects individuals and cultures as much as possible, judgments distinguishing between right and wrong are essential to advance the universal core values that form the basis of a civilized society.

Self-Esteem Programs. The theory: If young people feel good about themselves, then they will act good. The reality: No evidence supports this idea, and the risk is that we simply separate how we feel about ourselves from how we behave. Such programs tend to emphasize *feeling* good over *being* good.

Not all people of character have high self-esteem, and not all people with high self-esteem have good character. Abraham Lincoln and Winston Churchill were both known to have low self-esteem and to wrestle with chronic depression. Yet their strong character is well-known and was based on their behavior. Character education addresses one's worth in terms of more objective and universal (rather than purely personal) criteria of virtue.

Accepting oneself and having high self-esteem are obviously important. However, it is not enough that one clarify personal values. To develop strong character in young people, we must recognize some values as inherently superior to others (e.g., kindness over selfishness). Likewise, we must rank ethical values above personal preference and pragmatic values. The character of an individual and the quality of our society depend on the ethical content of the values we choose to live by.

Teaching by Example Alone. Another approach to character education is that of teaching solely by example. The assumption is that if young people see good character, they will imitate it. The flaw in this approach is that examples alone can send ambiguous messages. For instance, when someone holds a door open for a person of the opposite sex, does that behavior arise from respect and politeness or from sexual attraction? While modeling good character is vital, without a context — that is, without some training in what good character is and does — mere teaching by example fails.

Direct Teaching Plus Example. Effective character-building programs should be concrete, explicit, pervasive and repetitive. The messages sent should be direct and unambiguous about the nature and importance of ethical values. Modeling and examples of ethical behavior and good character should then accompany and be consistent with these messages.

Decline in the Health of the Family Structure. The integrity of the family structure, the first ingredient in promoting strong character, came under attack shortly after World War II. Changes in transportation and communication costs, corporate structure and workplace expectations, increased the mobility of families while decreasing the stability needed for healthy family and character development. Nuclear families became separated from extended families. Increasingly, both parents went to work and spent more time away from home than ever before. The result was a skyrocketing divorce rate that has obviously had a negative impact on all involved, but especially on the children of divorce. Custody battles and visitation problems often resulted in guilt, permissiveness and anger, which permeated the core of many chronically stressed families. Consequently, anxiety, depression and suicidal tendencies increased and left our youth more susceptible to the outside influences of peers, the media, and mood-altering substances and events (Brooks & Goble, 1997; Lickona, 1992).

The "me decades" of the 1960s, 70s and 80s significantly promoted the philosophy of personalism. This focus on oneself "celebrated the worth, dignity and autonomy of the individual person, including the subjective self or inner life of the person. It emphasized rights more than responsibility, freedom more than commitment. It led people to focus on expressing and fulfilling themselves as free individuals rather than on fulfilling their obligations as members of groups such as family, church, community or country" (Lickona, 1992, p. 9).

In *The American Paradox*, David Meyers states that this era fostered the philosophy of: "Do your own thing. Seek your own bliss. Challenge authority. If it feels good, do it. Shun conformity. Don't force your values on others" (Meyers, 2000, p. 7).

This period of self-entitlement also spawned unembarrassed assertions of "what's in it for me?" Schools took on driver education and let go of character education. It was a time of social recession, and as we lost our resolve to teach shared values, character itself waned. We were left with more questions than answers. "Is there an absolute right and wrong? Are all cultures, and their values, moral equals? Does someone have a right to presume moral judgments — and impose them on our children? Should we instead merely help students wrestle with moral dilemmas and clarify their personal values? Or, despairing of any consensus, should we avoid the subject, leaving values, virtues and character to the home?" (Meyers, 2000, p. 237)

The Desensitizing Effects of TV, Music, Movies and Video Games. Many social scientists believe that the media came to exert more power on youth in these unstable times. Television, movies and video games let children absorb endless scenes of violence, inappropriate sexuality and brutal empowerment. For example, to win many video games, one must manipulate the computer to maim, disfigure and kill others on the screen. "It seems incomprehensible that anyone would say that a seven-, 10- or 15-year-old is not desensitized to violence after watching, hour after hour, this graphic mayhem" (Brooks & Goble, 1997, p. 59).

Decline in the Influence of Religion. While American churchgoing is considerably higher than in other developed nations, it has declined in recent years. Putnam reported that "between 1974 and 1996, membership in church-related groups fell by at least 20 percent. Americans' involvement in the social life of their religious institutions apart from formal worship services has fallen, probably by one-third since the 1960s and by one-half or more since the 1950s" (2000, p. 72). The resulting struggle for economic survival caused many churches to soften their moral stance for fear of further attrition. During this same period, children and adolescents were less likely to become involved in church activities than their parents were. And when they did, even taking kids on field trips proved difficult because of insurance liability concerns (Brooks & Goble, 1997).

The Renewed Interest in Character Education

In the last century, seminal thinkers warned of the erosion of character. Alfred Adler, the Austrian psychiatrist whose ideas have gained influence since his death, stated that "social interest," a regard for the concerns of others, was the best barometer of mental health. Dr. Adler held that behavior is always purposeful and socially embedded. As a result, it is important to be socially responsible, cooperative and altruistic, and to be encouraged to make useful choices to achieve feelings of significance and belonging (Adler, 1956). American psychologist Abraham Maslow concurred, stating, "The ultimate disease of our time is valuelessness" (Gough, 1999). Lawrence Kohlberg, the famed developmental psychologist, also rejected the moral vacuity of values clarification and sought to help young people with the process of making ethical decisions (Lickona, 1992).

These concerns gained force in the later decades of the century. "If we, as parents, educators and community members, don't solve this character deficit problem," wrote David Brooks and Frank Goble, "we are doomed to live with the consequences. If we think that teen pregnancy, gangs, drug and alcohol abuse, school failure, a loss of civility, the lack of work ethic and violence are the problem, then we are doomed to live with these symptoms" (1997, p. 120).

The Aspen Declaration:
Articulating a National Framework for Character Education

In 1992, the Josephson Institute of Ethics hosted a three-day conclave of the nation's top experts in character education and representatives of many of the leading youth-serving and educational organizations. Their goal was to find ways to work together in order to amplify their efforts and increase their effectiveness. It soon became clear the first step was to develop a consensus on timeless, universal moral values, which could form the basis of a national framework for character education. They accepted the premise that good people can disagree on complicated social issues such as abortion and euthanasia, but believed there were some values that everyone could agree on. These values distinguish right from wrong and define the essence of good character.

The result was the Aspen Declaration, a seminal character development document consisting of eight principles about the nature, content and importance of character education, and articulating a common vocabulary of six core ethical values defining character (called the Six Pillars of Character): trustworthiness, respect, responsibility, fairness, caring and citizenship. The Aspen Declaration has since been adopted by thousands of national, regional and local organizations.

The Aspen Declaration

1. The next generation will be the stewards of our communities, nation and planet in extraordinarily critical times.

2. The present and future well-being of our society requires an involved, caring citizenry with good moral character.

3. People do not automatically develop good moral character; therefore, conscientious efforts must be made to help young people develop the values and abilities necessary for moral decision making and conduct.

4. Effective character education is based on core ethical values that form the foundation of democratic society, in particular, respect, responsibility, trustworthiness, caring, justice and fairness, and civic virtue and citizenship.

5. These core ethical values transcend cultural, religious and socioeconomic differences.

6. Character education is, first and foremost, an obligation of fami-

lies; it is also an important obligation of faith communities, schools, youth and other human-service organizations.

7. These obligations to develop character are best fulfilled when these groups work in concert.

8. The character and conduct of our youth reflect the character and conduct of society; therefore, every adult has the responsibility to teach and model the core ethical values and every social institution has the responsibility to promote the development of good character.

Notes

1. Lickona, T. (1992). *Educating for character: How our schools can teach respect and responsibility.* New York, NY: Bantam Books.

2. Bennett, W. (1992). *Devaluing of America.* New York, NY: Simon & Schuster, Inc.

3. Putnam, R. (2000). *Bowling alone.* New York, NY: Simon & Schuster.

4. Gough, R.W. (1998). *Character is destiny.* Rocklin, CA: Prima Publishing.

5. Brooks, B.D., & Goble, F.G. (1997). *The case for character education.* Northridge, CA: Studio 4 Productions.

6. Honig, B. (1986). From McGuffey's Reader to Johnny B. Goode, *School Safety News Journal.*

7. Meyers, D.G. (2000). *The American paradox.* New Haven, CT: Yale University Press.

8. Adler, A, (1956). *The individual psychology of Alfred Adler.* H.H. & R.R. Ansbacher, eds. New York, NY: Harper and Row.

The Advent of
CHARACTER COUNTS!

To translate the Aspen Declaration's principles into results, the Josephson Institute founded the **CHARACTER COUNTS!** Coalition in 1993. From 27 initial members, the Coalition now encompasses some 4,200 schools and many of the country's leading human-service agencies. It reaches more than five million youth and represents, by far, the nation's most widely implemented approach to character education.

Coalition members make three baseline commitments:

1. To integrate character development based on the Six Pillars of Character into new and existing programs.

2. To encourage young people and their parents to adopt and model these values through internal publications.

3. To collaborate with other Coalition organizations to develop context- and age-appropriate character-development materials.

CHARACTER COUNTS! is *not*:

- **A means to introduce religion or politics into public education**. The Six Pillars of Character are nonpartisan and nonsectarian, although they are also values taught in all major religions and across all national boundaries.

- **An "add-on" program. CHARACTER COUNTS!** is part of the fabric of classroom and school life, not an extra program that diverts attention from basic academic goals or weighs down already overburdened teachers. Both national teachers' unions as well as many national education associations endorse **CHARACTER COUNTS!** as a means of enhancing the school's ability to concentrate on traditional academic goals.

- **A fad solution.** CHARACTER COUNTS! is so basic, so commonsensical and so classic that it cannot be considered a "silver bullet" solution to a trendy issue. It is a carefully designed, long-term, community-based strategy to permanently embed character development goals in schools, youth organizations and communities.

- **A "feel-good" program.** CHARACTER COUNTS! does not stress empty self-esteem or personal happiness and success. It stresses the need to discern right from wrong and the acceptance of moral obligations. Self-respect stems from good choices and real accomplishment.

Theoretical Underpinnings

CHARACTER COUNTS! rests on important, solid theoretical bases:

The first foundation is indirect reciprocity theory, which science has shown explains much of cooperation and ethics itself. Indirect reciprocity takes place when Person A is kind (or unkind) to Person B, a third person observes it, and as a result acts kindly (or unkindly) to Person A. One researcher sums it up: "When they perceive that others are behaving cooperatively, individuals are moved by honor, altruism and like dispositions to contribute to public goods." People cooperate more with people who have a reputation for decency, and they cooperate to gain such a reputation themselves when others clearly value it (Alexander, 1979; Nowak & Sigmund, 1998).

A version known as strong reciprocity theory places more emphasis on rewards and punishments and creating a climate in which everyone is more likely to provide them. CHARACTER COUNTS! works to attain the state described by this theory, in which individuals reward fair and punish unfair behavior "even if this is costly and provides neither present nor future material rewards." Strong reciprocity is reciprocity combined with group-wide behavior modification. It can lead to near-maximal cooperation and is a powerful device for enforcing social norms (Fehr, Fischbacher & Gachter, 2002).

In **CHARACTER COUNTS!**, teachers and students discuss the Six Pillars regularly and the values become a common language. What are the consequences? Students see other students expressing decent opinions about the Pillars and become more likely to cooperate with them. Students who express such opinions develop better reputations for beneficence and receive more of it in turn. As the children treat each other better, they reciprocate directly more often. They trust each other, and their teachers, more. Their incidence of misbehavior falls and they become more diligent students, attending class and turning in homework more regularly. As reciprocity theory predicts, they behave better.

CHARACTER COUNTS! works toward the strong reciprocity state, where individuals make special efforts to reward good behavior and punish bad. In **CHARACTER COUNTS!** programs, teachers and youth leaders provide rewards and punishments indirectly, in comments about fictional characters, for instance, and directly, with rewards and discipline. Children reward each other with their good behavior, and are likely to punish each other by calling their attention to violations of the Six Pillar values.

The second foundation is behavioral modification theory, which goes back to psychologist Edward Thorndike in 1910. It is a deeply fleshed-out version of the carrot and the stick, and no one doubts its validity. Indeed, it has successfully treated childhood ailments such as obsessive-compulsive disorder, attention deficit/hyperactivity disorder, phobias and separation anxiety disorder. Its two main tools are positive reinforcement, which fosters desired behaviors through rewards, and negative reinforcement, which deters unwanted behaviors by eliminating positive reinforcement or imposing penalties.

A good **CHARACTER COUNTS!** program uses both forms of reinforcement in its quest for strong reciprocity. Teachers and others dispense rewards — which can include "tickets" for showing good character, classroom honors and even prizes in the American Youth Character Awards. Teachers also frame discipline in terms of the Six Pillars, explaining which Pillars a student violated.

Central to effective reinforcement, also derived from behavior modification theory, is consistency of message and consistency of rewards and discipline. The ultimate goal, however, is to have youngsters become intrinsically motivated to be people of good character regardless of the consequences.

The third base is imitation theory. Scientists once dismissed imitation as a low-level ability, but it is cognitively difficult and people are far more adept at it than other creatures. Indeed, some scientists claim it enables empathy itself. It may also be basic for social learning, and it has major implications for "rationality," intelligence and culture. As USC professor Aude Billard says, imitation "is a fundamental means to relate socially to others, and people who are impaired in their imitative skills, such as people with autism, also show general impairment in other social skills" (Meltzoff & Decety, 2003).

CHARACTER COUNTS! makes serious use of the human propensity to imitate. In class, teachers apply the Six Pillars to, say, events from history or real-world math problems. Students absorb the method partly by imitation, internalizing it to use in other situations. Second, teachers, other adults and older students serve as role models. This aspect is essential, because children will imitate the behavior of adults. At the same time, of course, actions tell what older individuals really think of ethical standards. If actions stand at variance with words, children will believe the actions.

We often have to educate parents and teachers on the importance of modeling, and show them that the "do as I say and not as I do" approach doesn't work. Teachers have to internalize the values of CHARACTER COUNTS! and express them authentically for the program to succeed. Research has shown that CHARACTER COUNTS! is effective in creating internalization of the values by the adults teaching it. The entire school climate becomes more positive as educators strive to model the Six Pillars in every interpersonal relationship.

Fidelity to the Model

The CHARACTER COUNTS! Character Development Seminar (CDS) teaches people the Six Pillars of Character and effective strategies for using them. It emphasizes the need to pervade the school with the Six Pillars, in order to foster strong reciprocity and consistency, rather than setting aside separate time periods for instruction in character. All CDS trainings provide attendees with:

- A clear understanding of the moral norms — the Six Pillars — and their role in the lives of children and the adults who teach them.

- Realistic strategies for teaching and reinforcing these values. Teachers see how character education enhances, and needn't subtract time from, substantive course work.

- An understanding of the obstacles to introducing an aggressive character development program to a community — how to deal with apathy, skepticism, hostility, and political and religious concerns.

For CHARACTER COUNTS! to work, implementers should:

- Have 5-10 percent of the staff trained at a CDS.

- Set aside time for CDS graduates to communicate the model to the rest of the staff through in-service trainings and staff/department meetings.

- Have all adults understand the importance of their role as models and how to use the Six Pillars language in teachable moments with youth. Train all school staff, including bus drivers, cafeteria workers, custodians and front-office staff.

- Create a steering committee to implement and oversee the program.

- Work it into school improvement or strategic plans.

- Have the Six Pillars pervade the lesson plans and curriculum, rather than isolating them in separate instructional modules.

- Have the Six Pillars pervade all aspects of campus life, including student leadership activities, after-school and sports activities, discipline referral systems, and parent education and awareness programs.

- Keep the message, rewards and punishments consistent. Integrate these expected values and behaviors into discipline referral systems and recognition/awards programs.

These steps impact behavior. They color the environment with Six Pillar values and lead to an effective program.

As a result, children see others expressing good intentions and engage in indirect reciprocity. They act more ethically toward them. Children also see other children behaving better toward others — and toward themselves — and reward them further.

Children further respond to the consistent rewards and disciplinary actions embedded in the program. They understand the consequences of their behavior and know what they need to do to receive rewards and escape penalties. And since the reward-punishment system favors the Six Pillars, they tend to follow these values, and internalize them.

In addition, children imitate teachers and other adults (many of whom often say the program has improved their lives as well). They see teachers acting thoughtfully and emulate the behavior. They also see teachers interpreting actions in stories in terms of the Six Pillar values, for instance, and learn that vital skill as well.

CHARACTER COUNTS! acknowledges that there are other perspectives on how to define and develop character, that there are programs of great worth with different lists of values than the six developed in Aspen, and that even programs that propose no list of values at all can effectively stimulate character development. Nevertheless, the CHARACTER COUNTS! Coalition is committed to a strategy that magnifies the impact of character education through efforts to unify not just communities but the nation behind a list of specific consensus values. Therefore, CHARACTER COUNTS! does not generally distribute materials based on different lists of values because it would create confusion and dilute the impact of the common-language strategy.

CHARACTER COUNTS! recognizes that it is ineffective to even appear to impose a character education structure that does not reflect the values a community holds dear. There must be widespread "buy-in" of the core values. CHARACTER COUNTS! has found that the most effective process has four critical steps. A representative group should:

- Collect information on various approaches to character education. To help, the CHARACTER COUNTS! website (charactercounts.org) contains links to the websites of all known character education approaches and programs.

- Determine the attitudes and conduct it wants more and less of. These become the goals of the program you implement.

- Examine whether the Six Pillars of Character — trustworthiness, respect, responsibility, fairness, caring and citizenship — encompass the desired attitudes and behavior, and whether the group feels comfortable with the strategies and resources of CHARACTER COUNTS!.

- Finally, look at other approaches and determine which best meets the group's needs, or even whether it wants to develop its own unique program based on values derived from a more extensive process involving all the major constituencies of the organization or community.

Organizations and communities that find immediate merit in CHARACTER COUNTS! adopt it and move straight to implementation, while others engage in a more prolonged analytical process. Many of the latter ultimately decide to use CHARACTER COUNTS!, and still others create their own programs.

Some character educators believe that each entity should develop its own list of virtues. While we do not recommend this approach, we do not oppose it either and it is not inherently incompatible with the overall goals of CHARACTER COUNTS!. Our differences in this area with a few character educators are matters of strategy, not substance.

When we deal with organizations that want to make their own lists, we simply caution them to be alert for the following problems:

- Overemphasis on "process" can drain energies and widen differences. Sometimes it becomes so lengthy or politicized that it delays the crucial implementation phase of character education.

- It also focuses on making lists and lobbying for consensus rather than getting on with the hard work of teaching core values like respect and responsibility.

- The task can yield long lists of virtues that are redundant or overlapping, and are too difficult to include in an effective program.

- Because of the influence of a few people, the list may contain controversial values (e.g., faith, obedience, reverence, patriotism) that could divide the organization and create opposition to the program, especially in public schools.

- A strong person in the group can influence others who seek consensus to accept particular words though there is no true buy-in. Hence the process may produce compromise rather than true consensus. This can weaken the program.

- The buy-in may not extend beyond the small group that made the list. Others may demand repetition of the process, and numerous iterations may each yield a different list.

- The logic of "make your own list" justifies each school making a list in a way that guarantees no uniformity of message even in the same school district. And when new people appear (such as principal, PTA president, parents), the old list is not "theirs" and they treat it as someone else's.

- The process leads to numerous possible lists and thus reinforces ethical relativism, the perception that ethics is just a matter of opinion and culture. **CHARACTER COUNTS!** believes the Six Pillars of Character are universal values applicable to all people, whether they list them or not. We have seen lists with glaring omissions.

A statute authorizing funds for character education should articulate the specific values it wants to promote. Without a list of core values proven to be acceptable and effective, legislators would be in effect signing a blank check to fund programs that could invite divisive controversy by listing values that are not universally accepted. Funding legislation should also overtly encourage collaboration to avoid fragmentation of efforts.

Public money should accomplish important purposes efficiently. The key public purpose of character education is a citizenry of good character. Therefore, legislatures should spend funds only on programs with proven track records of success, both in garnering community support and in delivering strategies that really work. Listing the six core values is one way to accomplish this.

Listing the six core values fosters more meaningful national evaluations of programs. Without a common list, it would be very difficult to compare programs and assess their impact.

Notes

1. Alexander, R.D. (1979). *Darwinism and human affairs.* Seattle, WA: University of Washington Press.

2. Nowak, M.A. & Sigmund, K. (1998). Evolution of indirect reciprocity by image scoring. *Nature, 393,* 573-577.

3. Fehr, E., Fischbacher, U., & Gachter, S. (2002). Strong reciprocity, human cooperation and the enforcement of social norms. *Human Nature, 13,* 1-25.

4. Meltzoff, A.N. & Decety, J. (2003). What imitation tells us about social cognition. *Philosophical Transactions of the Royal Society of London, 358,* 491-500.

The CHARACTER COUNTS! Approach

CHARACTER COUNTS! cultivates ethical behavior among everyone, but it especially helps adults shape children into adults of integrity. An initiative of the Josephson Institute of Ethics in Los Angeles, CHARACTER COUNTS! (CC!) is by far the most widely implemented character education framework in the nation. Well over five million youths come into regular contact with it, through the more than 560 school districts, communities and youth-serving organizations that form the CHARACTER COUNTS! Coalition. Over 4,200 schools embrace CHARACTER COUNTS!, including those in Albuquerque, Dallas, Knoxville, Akron, Mobile and Los Angeles. Cities, counties and entire states like Arizona have implemented it. And through its presence in the Child & Youth Services of the United States Army, it touches children worldwide.

In addition to schools and school districts, the Coalition embraces nationwide organizations such as Big Brothers Big Sisters of America, the American Red Cross, Little League Baseball, the American Youth Soccer Organization, National 4-H, the American Federation of Teachers, Boys & Girls Clubs of America, YMCA of the USA, the NEA, the National Association of Secondary School Principals and United Way of America. Other members include community organizations and local government agencies, such as the City of Nashville and Fairfax County, Virginia.

How It Works

CHARACTER COUNTS! employs a framework with many tiers: values, adult behavior, means of inculcation and results.

The first level of the framework deals with values, expressed in the Six Pillars of Character: trustworthiness, respect, responsibility, fairness, caring and citizenship. These are values accepted in every culture and across the political and religious spectrums. Each Pillar can embody other principles, so they sum up most ethical values, and CC! defines the Pillars in all their complexity. They are the backbone of the program:

- **Trustworthiness** involves being honest, sincere, forthright and candid; having the integrity to discern what's right and the moral courage to act on it; keeping promises; being dependable and prepared; and having loyalty to stand by, stick up for and protect one's family, friends, workplace and country.

- **Respect** entails honoring the individual worth and dignity of others, showing courtesy and civility, honoring reasonable social standards and customs, living by the Golden Rule, accepting differences, judging on character and ability, respecting the autonomy of others, and avoiding actual or threatened violence.

- **Responsibility** involves being accountable, exercising self-control, setting goals, choosing a positive attitude, doing one's duty, being self-reliant, pursuing excellence, being proactive, being persistent and reflective, setting a good example, and being morally autonomous.

- **Fairness** entails impartiality, thorough gathering of facts, and considering all perspectives before making a judgment.

- **Caring** involves compassion, empathy, kindness, consideration, charity, sacrifice, gratitude, mercy and forgiveness, altruism, generosity and sharing.

- **Citizenship** involves obeying the law, doing one's share, pursuing the common good, protecting the environment, obeying authority and honoring the principles of democracy.

The second tier of the framework deals with adult behavior. CHARACTER COUNTS! calls it T.E.A.M., for Teach, Enforce, Advocate and Model. Adults must:

- **Teach** children that their character counts, explaining that their success and happiness depend on who they are inside, not on what they have or how they look. Adults teach them the difference between right and wrong, and help them guide their thoughts and actions by the Six Pillars of Character, explaining these words with examples from the immediate surroundings, history and the news.

- **Enforce** the Six Pillars of Character, rewarding good behavior (usually praise is enough) and discouraging bad behavior by imposing fair, consistent consequences (or allowing others to). Adults demonstrate courage and firmness of will by enforcing these core values even when it is difficult and costly to do so.

- **Advocate** character, continually encouraging children to live up to the Six Pillars. Adults aren't neutral about the importance of character or casual about improper conduct. They are clear and uncompromising that they expect young people to be trustworthy, respectful, responsible, fair, caring and good citizens.

- **Model** good behavior. Everything adults say and do (or neglect to) sends a message about their values, so they make sure these messages reinforce their lessons about doing the right thing even when it is difficult. When they slip, they are accountable. They apologize sincerely and strive to do better.

The means of inculcating the Six Pillars of Character have six elements. The means must be:

- **Purposeful.** Activities aim deliberately at demonstrating the Six Pillars.

- **Pervasive.** The program permeates the school or organization, and ideally the whole community.

- **Repetitive.** Teachers, coordinators and others repeat the Six Pillars so the values become meaningfully ingrained in children's minds.

- **Consistent.** Organizations and individuals deliver an unswerving message at every level, and dispense rewards and punishments in a regular, predictable way.

- **Creative.** Teachers use their imagination to infuse the Six Pillars into activities in an interesting way, and develop new activities entirely.

- **Concrete.** Adults relate the Six Pillar values to easily visualized cases, so children can see how they play out in real-world terms.

Finally, the desired outcome of the process is for each student to become *conscious* of, *committed* to, and *competent* at using the Six Pillars:

- **Consciousness.** Children grasp the many dimensions of each Pillar principle.

- **Commitment.** Children internalize the importance of these values and adhere to them in daily life.

- **Competence.** Children are able to make successful decisions in real life using the Pillars as a decision-making guide.

CC! Is Research-based and Meets NCLB Requirements

The No Child Left Behind (NCLB) Act of 2001 calls for educational activities and programs to be supported by scientifically-based research. Scientifically-based research involves the application of rigorous, systematic and objective procedures to obtain a reliable and valid assessment of educational activities and programs. Since 1997 researchers at South Dakota State University have been studying the effectiveness of **CHARACTER COUNTS!** in schools throughout the state. The following information applies to this research. (Later in this document you can read more about **CHARACTER COUNTS!** results, including from South Dakota.)

Systematic and Empirical Methods

- Does the research have a solid theoretical foundation? YES

- Were methodology, subject and researcher clearly identified? YES

- Was the study conducted in a consistent, disciplined and methodical manner? YES

- Was the data obtained using observation or experiment? YES

- Was the research grounded in data that are factual rather than option-based? YES

- Are the research findings supported by tangible, measurable evidence? YES

Rigorous Data Analysis

- Did the research test the stated hypotheses and justify the general conclusions drawn? YES

- Did the methods correspond to the nature and structure of the data? YES

- Did the research minimize alternative explanations for observed effects? YES

- Did the research findings present convincing documentation that the observed results were caused by the intervention? YES

Reliable and Valid Data Collection

- Did the data result from a study involving multiple investigations in a number of locations? YES

- Were research biases minimized? YES

- Was the data measured consistently? YES

- Did repeated measurements on subjects taken under similar circumstances produce similar results? YES

Strong Research Design

- Do the controls allow for the evaluation of the condition(s) of interest? YES

- Was the study designed to optimize the investigator's ability to answer the research question? YES

- Does the design describe a random assignment experiment in which subjects are assigned to different conditions with appropriate controls? NO [Note: There was a control group in the initial research design, but the control group schools asked to be part of the **CHARACTER COUNTS!** initiative. More studies are in process and will be forthcoming.]

Detailed Results That Allow for Duplication

- Are the findings clearly described and reported? YES

- Are the results of the research sufficiently detailed so that replication of the design is possible? YES

- Can the findings be enhanced with additional research? YES

Results Subjected to Scrutiny

- Has the research been accepted by a peer-reviewed journal or approved by a panel of independent experts? PENDING: The research is currently under review.

- Have unbiased experts who were not a part of the research study reviewed the research? YES

- Have reviewers applied strict standards of scholarship and provided quality controls for the research they reviewed? YES

- Has the research been subjected to external verification? YES

How You Participate

To educate people in these frameworks and ensure the quality and sustainability of **CHARACTER COUNTS!**, the Josephson Institute conducts extensive training programs for teachers and other youth-serving professionals. The three-day courses, called Character

Development Seminars (CDS), prepare these individuals to teach ethical decision making based on the Six Pillars and show how to start **CC!** programs in schools or communities. These are train-the-trainer courses and have a multiplier effect in communities. Though **CHARACTER COUNTS!** is a national program, it works at the grassroots level and is self-supporting there.

The Institute brings **CHARACTER COUNTS!** to organizations in three stages: training, implementation and ongoing education. Youth-serving professionals take part in our Character Development Seminars, launch **CHARACTER COUNTS!**, and then sustain it, drawing on the resources of the national office as they see fit.

First Phase: Training

At the outset, educators or other personnel attend a Character Development Seminar, the cornerstone of **CHARACTER COUNTS!**. Highly qualified national faculty members — all certified by the Institute and very experienced at building character education programs in their own schools or communities — teach these high-intensity, small group workshops. Attendees learn the **CHARACTER COUNTS!** framework, methods and strategies for promoting good character, and they become equipped to develop a strategic plan in the school and community. More than 9,000 people have now completed CDS's and become certified character development specialists. By training small groups of school personnel to teach others ("training the trainers"), the CDS enables them to effectively spread **CHARACTER COUNTS!**.

Second Phase: Implementation

Next, graduates return to the school and teach the remaining staff — teachers, counselors and education leaders — character development theory and practical strategies using the Six Pillar framework. The teachers merge Six Pillar values into daily lessons, using suggestions from the CDS as well as publications like our popular *Good Ideas* book of lesson and activity plans and the *CHARACTER COUNTS!*

Chronicle newsletter. Indeed, in a school **CHARACTER COUNTS!** pervades the curriculum, the discipline referral system, after-school activities — everything that happens on campus. And since teachers work at the grassroots level, they can tailor the program to their needs. For instance, a **CHARACTER COUNTS!** initiative on a reservation might link the Six Pillars to tribal values. Teachers and steering committees also spread **CC!** to families and the community, so it pervades the environment. Students thus absorb the six core ethical values into their everyday decision making.

Third Phase: Ongoing Education

Finally, the Institute offers an array of follow-up tools to keep **CHARACTER COUNTS!** programs healthy and effective. It provides extensive printed PowerPoint presentations and other bound material to help a school or community conduct ongoing training locally. It offers consultation for teachers and support staff. It provides a listserv and other e-mail communications to keep practitioners aware of best practices. The Institute's representatives make check-in calls and stay in communication by e-mail with graduates. It regularly sends out informative newsletters: the **CHARACTER COUNTS!** *Chronicle*, the *Pursuing Victory With Honor Sportsmanship Newsletter* and Michael Josephson's weekly *Commentaries*. Its three websites — charactercounts.org, josephsoninstitute.org and FFL-essays.org (for its Foundations for Life essay program) — are a trove of free information. The Institute provides further training, especially through its one-day staff in-services and the Character Development Masters class, which directly addresses sustainability. It offers referral services and sharing mechanisms. Finally it has certified 115 Ethical Communities across the country, to provide continuity beyond school and a broad ethical context.

The Results Are In:
CHARACTER COUNTS! Works

CHARACTER COUNTS! has become the most influential force in character education for a good and simple reason — it works. It moves more easily to more venues than any other character-education strategy. Most importantly, it has proven its success. Here's a round-up of examples:

CHARACTER COUNTS! transformed South Dakota schools, according to a South Dakota State University study of up to 8,000 middle and high school students. It showed that:

CHARACTER COUNTS! cuts delinquency. After three years of exposure to **CC!**, students who said they had:

- Broken into another's property dropped 50 percent.

- Used a fake ID dropped 56 percent.

- Taken something without paying dropped 46 percent.

- Used physical force against someone who insulted them dropped 33 percent.

- Defaced or vandalized property dropped 46 percent.

- Drunk alcoholic beverages dropped 31 percent.

- Taken illegal drugs dropped 32 percent.

CHARACTER COUNTS! strengthens commitment to school. In South Dakota, it led to changes one would expect from greater commitment to school. Students who said they had:

- Cheated on an exam dropped 30 percent.

- Missed class without a legitimate excuse dropped 39 percent.

- Failed to get schoolwork done on time dropped 24 percent.

- Lied to a teacher dropped 35 percent.

CHARACTER COUNTS! enhances the social climate. "It's like night and day," said Linda Jones, who oversaw CC! in the Dallas public schools. "The whole emotional atmosphere of the building changes. It becomes a kinder, gentler place." For example, after CHARACTER COUNTS!, South Dakota students who said they had:

- Teased someone because of race or ethnicity dropped 45 percent.

- Received a detention or suspension dropped 28 percent.

Formal teacher observations corroborate these figures.

In fact, major changes appeared in South Dakota even after one year. Vandalism dropped 35 percent, property break-ins fell 42 percent, theft declined 34 percent, use of alcoholic beverages declined 21 percent, use of illegal drugs fell 18 percent, use of fake ID's fell 33 percent, and use of physical force in response to an insult fell 31 percent (Moss & Walsh, 2001).

Elsewhere, CHARACTER COUNTS! has also brought dramatic improvements in behavior. For instance:

- "The first year I was here we had over 1,500 discipline referrals," said principal Marcell Archer of John J. Pershing Elementary School, Dallas, in 2004. Then CHARACTER COUNTS! arrived. "This year, we probably don't have even 100."

- Discipline referrals fell 75 percent at Easton Elementary (grades 2-5) in Easton, Maryland, over the four years of CHARACTER COUNTS!. "And attendance is the highest in the county," says principal Kelly Griffith.

- School-related youth offenses have dropped 74 percent in St. Johns County, Florida, since CC! began there in 1998-99. By comparison, in next-door neighbor Flagler County — a near-clone of St. Johns but without CHARACTER COUNTS! — they dropped just nine percent.

- CHARACTER COUNTS! almost eliminated recidivism in a modified "boot camp" at the Tulare County Probation Youth Facility in California. Just 8 percent of its youths committed crimes in post aftercare, compared to a national rate of 72 percent. Only 30 percent of the youths committed crimes in residence — compared to a national average of 64 percent.

Cherie Townsend has seen this effect firsthand, as director of the Maricopa County Juvenile Court System in Arizona. "Initially, I was very skeptical about doing character education," she says. "I believed that this is something you teach within families." Finally, unconvinced, she agreed to pilot a program. "I was amazed," she says. "The Pillars are a very solid foundation with a very broad application. Our incidents in detention have gone down and I attribute that to the implementation of the CHARACTER COUNTS! curriculum" (Fry & McNeill, 2004).

CHARACTER COUNTS! can also improve academic performance. Few studies have yet investigated this important relationship, but the principal of Atlantis Elementary in Port St. John, Florida reported academic improvements after implementing CC!. Students scoring at level 3 (on an ascending scale of 1-5) on the Florida Comprehensive Assessment Test rose from 48 percent to 78 percent in one year. The average standard score in reading rose from 311 to 323 from 1998-2001, and in math the average standard score rose from 321 to 341 (Williams & Taylor, 2003).

Finally, CHARACTER COUNTS! leads to internalization of character traits by those who administer it — critical since young people imitate them. According to two scholars, teaching CC! led to "an increase in the likelihood of personal and professional development" (Harms & Fritz, 2001).

Notes

1. Moss, M. & Walsh, R. (2001). Results from the character education survey conducted in five counties throughout South Dakota. Brookings, SD: South Dakota State University 4-H Cooperative Extension.

2. Harms, K. & Fritz, S. (2001). Internalization of character traits by those who teach **CHARACTER COUNTS!** *Journal of Extension, 39, 6.*

3. Fry, P. & McNeill, D. (2004). Character really *does* count in schools throughout America. Los Angeles, CA: Josephson Institute of Ethics.

4. Williams, R.D. & Taylor, R.T. (2003). *Leading with character to improve student achievement.* Character Development Group.

Principles of Effective Character Education

Scholar Thomas Lickona argues that character development must start with a solid theory of good character and the school's goals. "Character must be broadly conceived to encompass the cognitive, affective and behavioral aspects of morality," he writes. "Good character consists of knowing the good, desiring the good, and doing the good. Schools must help children *understand* the core values, *adopt* or commit to them, and then *act upon* them in their own lives" (1993).

Knowing the Good. To know the good, a character program must enhance the ability to perceive and understand the moral dimension of behavior, to discern right from wrong through the application of ethical principles, and to make ethical decisions after considering the consequences to stakeholders and trade-offs between competing standards. Most people have positive instincts for caring and fairness, but beyond these basic instincts, knowing right from wrong and how to deal with conflicts among core ethical principles is not innate. The intellectual aspects of moral reasoning and decision making can and must be taught.

Wanting the Good. To want the good, a character program must contain elements that inspire and reinforce a desire to be a person of character, and to do what is right. In this stage, students develop an emotional commitment to being a good person and doing the right thing. They develop a durable and deep belief in the ethical principles they have been taught, and in the moral duty to be "good" and do "right." The commitment they develop to lead a meaningful "good" life is often spiritual in nature and goes beyond pure cost-benefit reasoning and logic.

Doing the Good. And finally, in doing the good, a character program deals with the habits and ethical behavior itself. At this stage, ethical behavior becomes automatic and instinctive. Honesty, respect and kindness become habits.

Based on these criteria, effective character-building programs:

- **Develop thinking and problem-solving skills.** They educate young people about core ethical standards (the Six Pillars of Character) and the ethical dimension and consequences of their behaviors and choices. Also, young people must receive guidelines, models and examples of how to solve ethical problems.

- **Inspire moral ambitions.** Young people should be motivated to want to do the right thing. While ethical behavior has both short- and long-term benefits, young people need to understand that virtue can be its own reward.

- **Impose positive and negative consequences.** Young people should be recognized and praised for good behavior and choices as well as warned or reprimanded for bad.

- **Instill habits.** Opportunities to practice ethical choices should be provided. Challenging young people to examine the ethical dimensions of what they see in the world around them should be a matter of course.

- **Model good conduct.** Young people need to be exposed to adults who practice good character in their own lives.

More on Values, Ethics and Character

Ethical issues confront us everyday: being asked to lie for a friend, passing along a juicy piece of gossip, finding ourselves in conversation with a bigot, receiving too much change at the store, using our position to take advantage of an employee, treating others in a way we would not tolerate for ourselves, being "creative" with work reports or accounting. How do people without enough (or any) moral or character training respond? That's a problem.

Character education is a bulwark against, and a curative response to, personal and social dysfunction. It's worth exploring the elements it seeks to address: values, ethics and character.

Values

Hank Hill is the lead male character in the popular prime time cartoon *King of the Hill*. One thing very important to Hank is his lawn. He takes great pride in its health and appearance, and great pains to make sure it's cut just right. He sees yard work as a privilege. To Hank, an appropriate punishment for his son Bobby is denying him the opportunity to mow. And of course, Hank is in competition with his neighbor about who has the best lawn in the neighborhood.

The trophy lawn — and the superiority and pride it represents — is a value for Hank. Values are the ideas, beliefs and desires that shape the formation of goals, motivate actions and establish criteria for evaluating decisions and conduct. Values help us interpret the world around us, detect the need for decisions, and make coherent ones. We all have values of some kind. We all use values every day to make choices and set priorities. For example, what causes us to get to work earlier or stay later than our colleagues? Why do we like to sleep in on Sunday mornings? If we examine our motives closely, all of these behaviors can be traced back to what we value. Because we have these values, we behave accordingly.

Ethical and Nonethical Values

Ethical Values. Values come in two categories: ethical and nonethical. Ethical values are what we believe is important regarding right and good, based on moral duty and virtues. Think about why we get upset with ourselves when we tell a lie or when we're lied to. Most often it's because trust and honesty are important to us. They are part of our ethical values.

Nonethical Values. Nonethical values refer to anything we think is important without reference to a moral quality or result. They are ethically neutral. For example, we plan for our retirement by setting aside a certain amount of money each month for investment. It is neither right or wrong to do this, but most would agree that it is important.

The Formation of Values

Conditioning and Reinforcement. A major source of values is conditioning and reinforcement. For instance, we are conditioned by the direct and implied teaching of parents, teachers, clergy, youth organization leaders, neighbors, cultural beliefs, television, music, movies and other sources regarding what is right, desirable and effective.

Socialization. We also grew up watching the behaviors of others. Social learning and modeling helped shape which behaviors we value as we witnessed numerous choices and their consequences. As a result, we developed certain response patterns. Core beliefs regarding what we value become more ingrained via life experiences, and thoughts become more automatic as behaviors yield predictable emotional consequences.

Temperament. Temperament also influences values. Sensitive people are often more inclined to be caring. Rational individuals may have a greater propensity for honesty.

The Power to Choose Our Values. Regardless of temperament or social learning, however, we have the power to choose freely. This is due to our ability to reason and develop a decision-making process based on values related to our belief system and resulting personal and professional goals.

Three Important Facts About Values

Many Personal Values Are Wants or Ideals. Many of our "values" are simply the way we think things should be if the world were run according to us. Wouldn't it be nice if all the traffic lights turned green just for us so that we could get to work on time after sleeping in that extra 15 minutes? Wouldn't we like all our investments to grow? Most people's idea of a "perfect" world is one where all of their wants were satisfied. We know that life doesn't operate that way, but we still find ourselves frustrated when what we think is important is ignored or overlooked by others or by circumstances.

Values Are Ranked by Importance. These rankings are our value system, which determines our priorities. That is, our value system determines how we behave in certain situations. Let's suppose we are driving home when we notice a tall apartment building on fire. As we get closer we see that the fire is terrible, and that children at one window are screaming for help. Certainly no one wants to see children die, but how many people would run into a burning building to save unknown youngsters? Now let's change one fact: suppose they are our children. Important new values would enter the situation. Wouldn't they change our priorities and our behavior?

Values Give Meaning. Values are what we feel is important, so they shape the goals in our lives, and how we measure our successes or failures. For example, suppose being successful is important to us, and that we define success this year as making $100,000.00. We work very hard and long, and things seem to be going very well. But at the end of the year, we have made only $98,000.00. Are we a success or a failure? How we define ourselves in that situation depends on our values. It doesn't matter what others may say about our achievements. Our values determine how we view them.

Ethics

Ethics is not about the way things are; it is about the way things *ought* to be. Ethics is a set of standards of duty and virtue, and right and wrong that indicate how we should behave. While values determine what is important to us, ethical standards guide how we ought to pursue our goals. For example, we may really like (value) money or good grades. But do we gain them honorably or by theft (cheating)? Our ethics are the expression of how we pursue our values.

Ethics has three equally important aspects: discerning right from wrong, concern with stakeholders, and the discipline to do the right thing.

First, discernment is the recognition of what is right. It can be hard, since ethical principles do not always yield a single "moral" choice. Often there is more than one "right" way to respond, and these responses may conflict. In general, this conflict among different "right" responses is the source of most modern controversial issues, and the chosen "solution" often comes back to an individual's value system.

Second, stakeholders are all those affected by our ethical choices. We can't always arrive at justice and proper behavior by considering just the interaction between two people. We must often consider the impact on others.

Third, we need the discipline to do what is right, regardless of temptations and pressures to do otherwise. We must recognize the difference between stated and operational values. Stated values are what we *say* we value. Operational values are what we *actually* value as revealed by our actions and decisions, and how we resolve conflicts between competing values. Consistency between stated and operational values is a key ingredient of integrity.

Ethics Is About Doing Less Than the Permissible

We often say ethics is about doing the right thing, but sometimes it can be about self-restraint, not doing anything. An act is not proper simply because it is permissible or legal. Sometimes we should not do what we have the power to do.

Larissa was the team leader of four teachers preparing a lecture presentation for an educational convention. She was in charge of assigning the duties and the lectures to each of the teachers and for herself. She quickly went through the schedule and topics, and chose the time periods and topics that she felt would give her lots of exposure and would be most complimentary for her. The rest of the time periods and topics she handed out randomly among the other team members. Needless to say, they were not too happy when they realized what she had done.

Larissa was within her authority to act as she did. She didn't break any rules or laws. But the ethical thing would have been for her *not* to do what she obviously wanted to do.

Ethics Is About Doing More Than Necessary

Compliance is about doing what you are required to do by laws or rules. Ethics is about doing what you should do because it is right. An ethical person often chooses to do more than the law requires and less than the law allows. Ethics goes beyond compliance.

Consider the story of the old man charged with stealing food for his family and standing before a judge. "I have to punish you," the judge said. "The law is clear in this case, and I fine you 10 dollars." Then the judge pulled 10 dollars out of his own wallet and said, "The fine is paid. I now fine everyone in the courtroom fifty cents apiece for living in a town where a man has to steal in order to eat." The judge then placed a dollar bill in a hat, and started it around the room. After everyone paid the "fine," the judge called the old man over and handed him the $47.50.

Sometimes being compassionate is more ethical than keeping a rule. Certainly the judge has the responsibility to uphold the law, but this judge also wanted to do a greater good.

Unfortunately, we often balk at going further than the rules require. We adopt an attitude of "I'm not going to do more than they tell me to." So our work may comply with what was demanded, but it isn't really good work. Our adherence to safety regulations is faultless, but we don't bother removing an obvious hazard because "it's not part of my job." We comply, but our behavior is less than ethical.

Some even try to distort the meaning of compliance. A mother was angry with her son because there was only one cookie left in the cookie jar. He replied, "You told me I couldn't eat one cookie before supper. That's the one I didn't eat." Many people approach rules with the same attitude. They look for ways of fulfilling the letter, but not the spirit. For them, the paramount questions are: "How can I get around this rule?" and "What exactly can I get away with?"

Ethics Is Not About Self-Interest

Many people adopt a live-and-let-live attitude about behavior: "I'll do what I want and you do what you want. You don't judge me and I won't judge you."

Decision making is reduced to risk/reward calculations: if the risk is low enough or the rewards are great enough, they can jettison ethical principles and do what they think will benefit them most immediately.

Many people who cheat on exams, lie on resumes, or distort or falsify facts at work are never caught. So the ethics of self-interest, at least in the short run, may seem to work. But the long-term risks are loss of trust, broken relationships and loss of opportunities. Ironically, such a focus on self-interest is not in our self-interest.

Furthermore, what we say and do affects others around us. We all teach the values we demonstrate with our choices, attitude and behavior.

The real test of ethical character is whether we are willing to do the right thing even when it's not in our self-interest or when it costs more than we want to pay.

Some people believe that the pursuit of happiness is a moral end in itself. They argue that our values — what we prize and desire — determine what makes us "happy," and what makes us "happy" is what we should pursue. This is not unreasonable or unethical unless it is applied without regard to how others are affected by how we pursue our own happiness.

One of the greatest obstacles to being a person of character and leading an ethical life is the dominance of self-centered, pleasure-seeking values: doing what makes us "feel good," satisfying our passions and urges, and avoiding pain and discomfort at all costs. The morally mature individual finds happiness in grander pursuits than the temporary pleasure produced by money, status, popularity, sex or drugs.

Why Be Ethical?

- *Virtue Is Its Own Reward.* True self-esteem comes from the confidence and experience gained from accomplishing a task, including character tasks. Knowing that we have done the "right thing" makes us feel good about ourselves. The additional benefits are the admiration of loved ones and the trust and respect of peers.

- *It's the Smart Thing to Do.* Mark Twain once said, "If you tell the truth, you don't have to remember anything." In the long run, being ethical is simpler (if not always easier).

- *Religious Reasons.* If we are committed to a religion, ethical behavior complements our faith.

- *Habit.* Ethical choices comply with our upbringing or training.

Character

Everyone has a character — a bundle of habits, traits and predilections. But not everyone is of *good* character, someone who knows the difference between right and wrong, and consistently acts on that knowledge.

A singular act of virtue does not necessarily define our character. Take Bill, for example. Bill joined the Army during the Vietnam War to avoid arrest for his involvement in a robbery. He wasn't a very good soldier, but made good friends with the other soldiers in his small unit. One evening, while his squad was on a routine patrol, they were ambushed. Everyone in the unit was wounded, and many were killed. When Bill saw his friends hurt or dead, he became so enraged that he beat off the attack by himself and saved the lives of the other remaining soldiers. He received the Medal of Honor. When his time in service was complete, Bill returned to his old neighborhood to pick up life where he left off. Six months later he was killed when he attempted an armed robbery of a bank.

On the other hand, a single act of bad behavior is also not the summation of our true character. Many people can cripple their reputations by single acts of bad behavior, but they may have been the result of momentary weakness, a bad decision or mistake that they could learn from.

Consider Sheryl. She had always been a good worker: reliable, punctual, knowledgeable, accurate and pleasant to deal with. Her co-workers liked her and trusted her. A position in management opened up, and Sheryl found herself in contention for it, along with another esteemed colleague, Tom. One day Sheryl's boss was upset because some detail had been overlooked and a sale had been lost. Impulsively, Sheryl blurted out, "Well, Tom should have taken care of that." She knew that Tom had nothing to do with this particular transaction. Sheryl's boss went to talk with Tom. The truth came out and Sheryl's reputation for integrity was damaged. She didn't get the promotion, either.

It may not be fair, but people will judge us based on our last worst act, even when that act is "out of character" for us.

Character, Conscience and Reputation

Our conscience is our internal source of ethical judgment. A working conscience has two parts: it makes us aware of the moral aspect of our conduct, and it urges us to prefer right over wrong. If character is how we act when we think no one is watching, conscience is the inner force that is always watching (and listening).

Character education assumes that students have consciences. This, of course, may not always be the case. Sociopaths may perceive the distinction a society makes between "right" and "wrong," but they just don't care (unless they stand to benefit). Character education basically doesn't address these rare individuals; it focuses instead on the overwhelming majority of people who can learn to "know the good, love the good, and do the good" (Lickona, 1992).

Reputation is what other people think you are. It's something all of us care about, even sociopaths, for it is a great determiner of our influence over events and other people. But reputation is not character. Think about it in Lincoln's formulation: Your character is the tree and your reputation its shadow. The tree is solid, but the shape and length of the shadow depend on the angle of light. If we pay too much attention to our reputation, we could lose sight of our character.

Imagine the girl who wants to be popular with everyone. When she is with one group of "friends," she likes what they like, she dresses the way they dress, she listens to the same music they do. But when she is with another group of "friends," she conforms to what they like. When individuals from each group meet, and this girl comes up in their conversation, what is going to be the result? Both are going to realize that this girl has been less than honest. Not only is her reputation going to suffer with both groups, but she has exposed her true character to them as well.

The Sources of Character

Character is not an inherited genetic disposition, nor is it forever determined by the environment. We have a large measure of control over our character because we can choose and develop our own habits. Some personality traits, like our mother's fiery temper, may be inherited. What we choose to do with it determines our character.

There are four basic sources of character: personal discipline, our thoughts, courage and determination.

- **Personal Discipline.** Are our choices rational or emotional? Have we considered the possible consequences to ourselves and others? Have we considered our long-term goals? It's easy to act impulsively. It's hard to pause and learn the habit of thinking a situation through before acting.

- **Monitoring and Cultivating Our Thoughts.** An old adage warns us not to hang around with negative people. Negative people are very good at seeing what's wrong and how something "cannot be done." What's worse is that if we associate with them long enough, we end up sounding and acting just like them.

  The same process holds true with our thoughts. There's an old saying that goes, "Watch your thoughts; they become words.

Watch your words; they become actions. Watch your actions; they become habits. Watch your habits; they become character. Watch your character; it becomes your destiny." If we fill our mind with "me only" or "whatever it takes to get ahead," we shouldn't be surprised when our behavior follows. We should take a look at the thoughts that pop into our head the next time opportunity or temptation comes our way. What do they say about our values, our priorities and our ethics? How can they be adjusted to reflect better character? Changing the way we think is a first, big step toward changing our character.

- **Courage.** It takes courage to live up to principle, and it takes courage to change. The "comfortable" thing about old habits and ways of thinking is that we do know how they turn out. We may not like the results, but at least they are familiar. But when we start new ways of responding and behaving, suddenly we find ourselves in unknown territory, and it can be frightening. Courage is not the absence of fear; it is learning to control fear instead of letting fear control us. It takes courage to continually work on our character.

  A strange thing happens when we change: the people we associate with often change too. When we change, we have stopped being "us" and they have to deal with a different person. Their responses can range from support to ridicule to confusion and even to extreme anger. It takes courage to continue working on our character when others are pressuring us to stay as we were.

- **Determination.** Finally, good character is developed with determination. As with any new activity, we will make a lot of mistakes at the beginning. We will feel the pull of old habits and ways of thinking telling us to respond in the old familiar ways. And don't forget those old friends and family members who are still interacting with us according to our former character. Determination to be better, to improve our character, is necessary to be successful.

Notes

1. Lickona, T. (1993). The return of character education. *Educational Leadership*, 51(3), 6-11.

2. Lickona, T. (1992). *Educating for character: How our schools can teach respect and responsibility.* New York, NY: Bantam Books.

A Closer Look at the Six Pillars of Character

The CC! approach to nonpartisan, nonsectarian character education centers on the Six Pillars of Character, a common-language vocabulary to facilitate teaching and promotion of ethical decision making. With a shared vocabulary people see what unites our diverse and fractured society and helps them communicate more easily about core values. The common lexicon helps us consistently process the ethical implications of decisions, both our own and others'.

The Six Pillars act as a set of filters through which to process decisions. Being trustworthy is not enough — we must also be caring. Adhering to the letter of the law is not enough — we must accept responsibility for our action or inaction.

The Pillars can help us detect situations where we focus so hard on upholding one moral principle that we sacrifice another — where, intent on holding others accountable, we ignore the duty to be compassionate; where, intent on getting a job done, we ignore how we carry it out.

In short, the Six Pillars can dramatically improve the ethical quality of our decisions, and thus our character and lives.

Pillar #1: TRUSTWORTHINESS

A trustworthy person is worthy of others' reliance and confidence. When people trust us, they give us greater leeway because they feel we don't need monitoring to assure that we'll meet our obligations. They believe in us and hold us in higher esteem. At the same time, trustworthiness means we must constantly live up to the expectations of others and refrain from even small lies or self-serving behavior that can quickly destroy our relationships.

Simply refraining from deception is not enough. Trustworthiness is perhaps the most complicated of the six core ethical values and encompasses a variety of qualities like honesty, integrity, reliability and loyalty.

Honesty

There is no more fundamental ethical value than honesty. But honesty is a broader concept than many may realize. It involves both communications and conduct.

Honesty in communications is expressing the truth as best we know it and not conveying it in a way likely to mislead or deceive. There are three dimensions:

- *Truthfulness*. Truthfulness is presenting the facts to the best of our knowledge. Many of us have heard fishermen tell stories of an amazing catch. And with each telling, the tale gets bigger and bigger. While that kind of exaggeration is probably harmless, if we exaggerated other facts we could easily cause people to believe something that is untrue and damaging. For instance, when we exaggerate about someone's behavior or choices, not only are we lying, but we could well end up harming that person's reputation — and our own.

  On the other hand, being wrong about facts is not the same thing as lying. Intent is the crucial distinction between lying and mere error, although honest mistakes can still damage trust insofar as they suggest sloppy judgment.

- *Sincerity*. Sincerity is genuineness, being without trickery or duplicity. It precludes all acts — including half-truths, out-of-context statements and even silence — that are intended to create beliefs or leave impressions that are untrue or misleading. The stereotype of lack of sincerity is the used car salesperson. Why is that? Because we suspect the salesperson is going to highlight the good qualities of every vehicle and omit anything bad, and may even lie to us.

- *Candor.* In relationships involving legitimate expectations of trust, honesty may also require forthrightness and frankness, imposing the obligation to *volunteer* information that another person would want to know. In some parts of the world, doctors do not tell terminally ill patients or their families about the prognosis. While some may argue that such doctors are trying to be merciful, if we only had six months to live we might want to know so we could make preparations and make crucial choices during the time left.

Honesty in conduct is playing by the rules and not stealing, cheating, practicing fraud, or using subterfuge or other trickery. Cheating is a particularly foul form of dishonesty because one not only seeks to deceive but to take advantage of those who are not cheating. It's a violation of both trust and fairness.

Not All Lies Are Unethical. Honesty is not an inviolate principle. Not all lies are unethical, even though all lies are dishonest. Occasionally, dishonesty is ethically justifiable. Obviously when the police lie in undercover operations or when one lies to criminals or terrorists to save lives, we understand that other important responsibilities outweigh the need to be truthful. Mild dishonesty may also be all right to advance the Pillar of caring. If at Christmas a young daughter gives her father a tie that he hates, he would be justified in telling her he liked it to avoid hurting her feelings. But don't kid yourself: ethically sanctioned lying must serve a clear moral purpose, and the risks of damage to trustworthiness remain. Goals which do *not* justify lying include hitting a management-pleasing sales target, winning a game, and avoiding a confrontation.

Integrity

The Dickens character Uriah Heep has become the clichéd version of a person without integrity: the hypocrite. On the outside, Uriah was overly civil and polite, and always ingratiating to everyone. But underneath, he was planning and plotting, always looking for a way to turn things to his own advantage. When his scheming is exposed, the reader feels a sense of satisfaction and justice. We don't like to see such people get away with their underhanded ways.

The word *integrity* comes from the same Latin root as *integer*, or whole number. Like a whole number, a person of integrity is undivided and complete. This means that the ethical person acts according to his beliefs, not according to expediency. He is also consistent. There is no difference in the way he makes decisions from situation to situation. His principles don't vary at work or at home, in public or alone.

Because he must know who he is and what he values, the person of integrity takes time for self-reflection, so that the events, crises and seeming necessities of the day do not determine the course of his moral life. He stays in control. He may be courteous, even charming, but he is never duplicitous. He never demeans himself with obsequious behavior toward those he thinks might do him some good. People trust him because they know who he is. What you see is what you get.

Watch out for these four enemies of integrity:

- Self-interest – Things we want

- Self-protection – Things we want to avoid

- Self-deception – Refusal to see a situation clearly

- Self-righteousness – An end-justifies-the-means attitude

Reliability (Promise-Keeping)

A young couple decided to save to buy a new refrigerator. They resolved to throw their spare change and any one dollar bills they had at the end of the day into a coffee can they kept in one of the kitchen cabinets. One day the wife was window-shopping and found a blouse on sale that she fell in love with. However, she knew that even on sale, the budget didn't allow her to buy it. But then she remembered that coffee can in the kitchen, and she began to think that she could "borrow" the money from it and replace it later. But she didn't want to tell her husband. She would just do it without him knowing, and it would be her little secret. Besides, she rationalized, he would like the way she looked in this blouse too.

When she went to the cabinet she found the can was almost empty, except for a note, written in her husband's handwriting: "I.O.U. $35 – used the money for some CDs." She was furious!

While there may be no viable legal remedy for a broken promise, trust-worthiness binds us to follow through when we give others our word. When we make promises or act in such a way that others reasonably rely upon our commitment, we undertake special moral duties. We accept the responsibility of making all efforts to fulfill our commitments.

Because promise-keeping is such an important aspect of trustworthiness, it is important to avoid:

- **Unwise commitments.** Before making a promise, consider carefully whether you are willing and likely to keep it. Think about future events that could make compliance undesirable or difficult. Sometimes the best promise is simply to do our best.

- **Unclear commitments.** Be sure that, when you make a promise, the other person understands what you are committing to do.

- **Bad-faith excuses.** Interpret your promises fairly and honestly. Don't try to rationalize noncompliance.

Loyalty

One teenager tells another, "Come on! You're my best friend! You tell your parents you're spending the night at my house, and I'll tell my parents I'm spending the night at your house. Then we'll go to the party and stay up as late as we want."

Some relationships — husband-wife, employer-employee, citizen-country — create an expectation of special allegiance, fidelity and devotion. Loyalty is a responsibility to promote the interests of certain people, organizations or affiliations. This duty goes beyond the normal obligation we all share to care for others, and it can create unusual pressures and conflicts.

In fact, loyalty is a tricky thing. Friends, employers, co-workers and others may demand that we rank their interests above ethical considerations. But no one has the right to ask another to sacrifice ethical principles in the name of a special relationship. Indeed, one forfeits a claim of loyalty when he or she asks so high a price for maintaining the relationship.

There are three aspects:

- **Need to prioritize loyalties.** So many individuals and groups make loyalty claims on us that we must rank our loyalty obligations in a rational fashion. For example, it's perfectly reasonable, and ethical, to look out for the interests of our children, parents and spouses, even if we have to subordinate our obligations to other children, neighbors or co-workers in doing so.

- **Safeguarding confidential information.** Loyalty requires us to keep some information confidential. When keeping a secret breaks the law or threatens others, however, we may have a responsibility to "blow the whistle."

- **Avoiding conflicting interests.** Employees and public servants have a duty to make all professional decisions on merit, unimpeded by conflicting personal interests. They owe ultimate loyalty to the public.

Pillar #2: RESPECT

Delia had been friends with the same group of kids for years. At the beginning of the sophomore year, her friends started to drink, but Delia didn't. Her friends started to think she was weird.

"Can't you have just one?" her friend Gabby asked her. "What's so bad about it?"

One night at a party, scared that her friends would dump her for not joining in, Delia had a beer. She felt self-conscious holding the can. She didn't like the taste. And she wasn't into drinking games, so she really felt uncomfortable, and she didn't like being around the kids who were drunk.

But the worst part was afterwards. She was angry with her friends and with herself. They talked her into doing something she really didn't want to do, and she let them. And she felt guilty. Not only did she know her parents would have been really disappointed in her drinking, but she had done something she really didn't believe in (Carter-Scott, 2001).

The Essence of Respect. The essence of respect is to show regard for the worth of people, including oneself. In the above example, Delia's friends didn't respect her choice not to drink. Because she was "different" from them, they placed less value on her. In the end, she also showed disrespect for herself by doing something she really didn't want to do.

Right to Dignity. People are not things, and everyone has a right to be treated with dignity. We certainly have no ethical duty to hold all people in high esteem, but we should treat everyone with respect, regardless of who they are or what they have done. We have a responsibility to be the best we can be in all situations, even when dealing with unpleasant people.

The Golden Rule. The Golden Rule — do unto others as you would have them do unto you — nicely illustrates the Pillar of respect. Respect prohibits violence, humiliation, manipulation and exploitation. It reflects notions such as civility, courtesy, decency, dignity, autonomy, tolerance and acceptance.

Civility, Courtesy and Decency. A respectful person is an attentive listener, although his patience with the boorish need not be endless (respect works both ways). Nevertheless, the respectful person treats others with consideration, and doesn't resort to intimidation, coercion or violence except in extraordinary and limited situations to defend others, teach discipline, maintain order or achieve social justice. Punishment is used in moderation and only to advance important social goals and purposes.

Dignity and Autonomy. How do we feel when others make important decisions for us? Even when others have the best intentions and are genuinely concerned about our well-being, we still want to be consulted about decisions that affect us, especially when we are the ones who should be making the decision in the first place! We may make the wrong decision, but others need to recognize it's our choice to make.

People need to make informed decisions about their own lives. Don't withhold the information they need. Allow all individuals, including maturing children, to have a say in the decisions that affect them.

Tolerance and Acceptance. Accept individual differences and beliefs without prejudice. Understand that tolerance doesn't mean we agree with or accept for ourselves another person's beliefs, behaviors or values. But we do accept his right to make those choices for himself, just as we claim the right to make our own choices.

Judge others only on their character, abilities and conduct.

Pillar #3: RESPONSIBILITY

Life is full of choices. Being responsible means being in charge of our choices and, thus, our lives. It means being accountable for what we do and who we are. It also means recognizing that our actions matter and we are morally accountable for the consequences. Our capacity to reason and our freedom to choose make us morally autonomous and, therefore, answerable for whether we honor or degrade the ethical principles that give life meaning and purpose.

Ethical people show responsibility by being accountable, pursuing excellence and exercising self-restraint. They exhibit the ability to respond to expectations.

Accountability

An accountable person does not see herself as a victim and doesn't shift blame or claim credit for the work of others. She considers the likely consequences of her behavior and associations. She recognizes the common complicity in the triumph of evil when nothing is done to stop it. She leads by example.

Pursuit of Excellence

The pursuit of excellence has an ethical dimension when others rely upon our knowledge, ability or willingness to perform tasks safely and effectively.

Diligence. It is hardly unethical to make mistakes or to be less than "excellent," but there is a moral obligation to do one's best, to be diligent, reliable, careful, prepared and informed.

Perseverance. Responsible people finish what they start, overcoming obstacles rather than surrendering to them. They avoid excuses such as "That's just the way I am," "It's not my job," or "It was legal."

Continual Improvement. Responsible people always look for ways to do their work better.

Self-Restraint

Responsible people exercise self-control, restraining passions and appetites (such as lust, hatred, gluttony, greed and fear) for the sake of longer-term vision and better judgment. They delay gratification if necessary and never feel it's necessary to "win at any cost." They realize they are as they choose to be, every day.

Pillar #4: FAIRNESS

The boss is always late for her appointments, whether with other employees or clients — everyone has to wait on her. But she demands that those employees or clients never make her wait for them. If they do, she gets angry and reminds them that "my time is important." Is the boss's behavior fair?

You've no doubt heard children say, "That's not fair!" Kids begin understanding fairness and unfairness at an early age, but being fair consistently or even knowing what is fair is a lifelong struggle.

Fairness involves issues of equality, impartiality, proportionality, openness and due process. Most people agree that it is unfair to handle similar matters inconsistently or to impose punishment that is not commensurate with the offense. The basic concept seems simple, even intuitive, yet applying it in daily life can be difficult. Fairness is another tricky concept, probably more subject to legitimate debate and interpretation than any other ethical value. Disagreeing parties tend to maintain that there is only one fair position (their own, naturally). But essentially fairness implies adherence to a balanced standard of justice without reference to one's own biases or interests.

Process

In *To Kill a Mockingbird*, the drama of the trial comes partly from the culture of prejudice against African Americans: no one expects the local attorney, Atticus Finch, to put much effort into defending a black man accused of raping a white woman. Readers and filmgoers experience genuine anger at the mobs and villains who violently oppose Atticus for seeking genuine truth and justice for his client. We understand that they are not being fair.

Process is crucial in settling disputes, both to reach the fairest results and to minimize complaints. A fair person scrupulously employs open and impartial processes for gathering and evaluating the information necessary to make decisions. Fair people do not wait for the truth to come to them; they seek out relevant information and conflicting perspectives before making important judgments.

Impartiality

Another requirement of fairness is impartiality — decisions and judgments should be made without favoritism or prejudice. In the above example, people assumed the black man was guilty simply because he was black. They didn't wait for evidence or facts of his guilt or innocence.

Equity

Equity requires that we take extenuating circumstances into account when making judgments. It's not always easy. Take, for example, abused spouses or children who kill their abusers. Common law has viewed this as murder, but more recently some have argued that the abuse is an extenuating circumstance justifying self-defense. Or consider affirmative action in universities. Should students be accepted strictly on the basis of their merit, or is past discrimination against a particular race an extenuating circumstances that should change the entrance requirements for people of that race? These questions have no easy answers, yet in the pursuit of fairness our society has to wrestle with them.

Pillar #5: CARING

Harold was thrilled that he just received a promotion and a substantial bonus. With his check in his pocket he rushed out, anxious to get home to share the news with his wife and two sons. Just before he got to his car, a desperately sad looking woman with a young baby asked him for a few dollars. She said her child had leukemia and was dying. Harold reached into his pocket for loose bills and pulled out his bonus check by accident. He looked at the poor woman and her baby, endorsed the check and pushed it in her hand, saying, "Use this to do what you can for your baby." The woman looked at the check with astonishment and thanked him.

When he got home he told his family what happened. Josh, his 16-year-old son, was disdainful. "I can't believe you gave her our money. You don't even know her and for all you know she was conning you." Evan echoed his brother's cynicism.

Loretta, Harold's wife, finally said, "Harold, congratulations on your promotion and your bonus. You're a good man, and I'm proud of you."

A week later, Josh brought to his father a newspaper article about a woman with a baby who had been scamming people near Harold's building. Harold looked at her picture and smiled.

Josh said, "What are you smiling about? You were cheated! She made a fool out of you."

Harold said, "Don't you see? This is wonderful news. It means her baby isn't dying."

If you existed alone in the universe, there would be no need for ethics. But it is impossible to be truly ethical and unconcerned with the welfare of others. That is because ethics is ultimately about good relations with other people. Caring is the very heart of ethics.

Sometimes it's easier to love "humanity" than it is to love people. We all know people who consider themselves "ethical," yet lack a caring attitude toward individuals, whom they tend to treat as instruments of their will. They rarely feel an obligation to be honest, loyal, fair or respectful except insofar as it is prudent for them. A person who really cares feels an emotional response to both the pain and pleasure of others. A person who really cares shows it through action. Tender feelings are not enough.

Of course, sometimes we must hurt those we care for, and some ethical decisions can cause pain. But one should consciously cause no more harm than is reasonably necessary to perform one's duties.

The highest form of caring is the honest expression of benevolence, or altruism. This is different from strategic charity. Gifts to charities to advance personal interests are a fraud. That is, they aren't gifts at all. They're investments or tax write-offs.

Caring people, like all ethical individuals, sometimes get taken advantage of. But compassion and caring will always do more good over the long run than cynicism in protecting our interests of the moment.

Pillar #6: CITIZENSHIP

Society has numerous problems we would like to see solved. When we see homeless people cuddling for warmth next to buildings, crack dealers selling drugs to kids, or litter on the beach, we ask, "Why doesn't somebody do something about this?" Citizenship challenges us to be that somebody.

Citizenship includes civic virtues and duties that prescribe how we ought to behave as part of a community. The good citizen knows the laws and obeys them, yes, but that's not all. He volunteers and stays informed on the issues of the day, the better to execute his duties as a member of a self-governing democratic society. He does more than his fair share to make society work, now and for future generations. This commitment to the public sphere can take many forms, such as conserving resources, recycling, using public transportation and cleaning up litter. The good citizen gives more than he takes. If he feels a law is immoral, such as segregation, he works to change it with open and peaceful tactics such as civil disobedience.

Remember Edward Hale's inspiring words: "I am only one, but still I am one. I cannot do everything, but still I can do something, and because I cannot do everything I will not refuse to do the something that I can do." The Pillar of good citizenship challenges us to look beyond our own self-interests and do something good for our community, city, state, nation and world.

Imagine what the world could be:

If There Were More Trustworthiness: What would the world look like if people were more trustworthy? Disclosure would be much more honest and authentic, and relationships would vastly improve. Individuals would feel much better as a result of sharing their thoughts and feelings, while the listener would not have to expend energy trying to figure out what the person was "really" saying. People would keep more promises. There would be less doubt regarding commitment, follow-up, arrival and departure times, and faithfulness. Loyalty would become more common, and individuals could confront interpersonal conflicts more proactively, fostering solutions and an action plan. Integrity would spread, as thoughts, words and deeds would be in concert with each other. The positive impact on every relationship — with friendships, spouses, colleagues, neighbors, communities and nations — would be extraordinary.

If There Were More Respect: Each person would treat others more as social equals regardless of physical appearance, race, cultural differences, gender or age. People would tolerate differences of opinion better even if they led to disagreements. Condescending remarks would grow scarcer, while active listening would become more common in every conversation. Good manners would be more typical and there would be less prejudice, harassment, manipulation or coercion.

If There Were More Responsibility: Every individual would try harder to be an excellent parent, spouse, significant other, friend, worker, community member and volunteer. People would be more responsible for managing their time in harmony with their priorities, including their spiritual, emotional and physical well-being. Sound choices would be more common. Laziness and indifference would decline. The world would reap the rewards of greater productivity with people flourishing by using their gifts for the benefit of society.

If There Were More Fairness: Equal opportunity would exist for more people. Oppression would decline, with increasing efforts toward more open trade and access to food, shelter and technology. More evaluations would be made on relevant criteria, in school, higher education and the workplace. Cooperation, interdependence and charitable giving would increase, and more nations would have access to education and decent employment. Consequences for undesirable behavior would be more consistent and fitting.

If There Were More Caring: People would seek out more ways to make a positive difference in the lives of others. Uncaring and hurtful remarks would decline. Many more positive statements and encouraging words would be offered while people were alive, rather than just at their funerals. More people would thrive in life, and there would be fewer cases of abuse, neglect and loneliness. Caring would also extend to one's self and career. Wellness, positive energy and a passion for living would be the by-product of a more caring climate.

If There Were More Good Citizenship: People would vote a greater number of politicians into office on appropriate criteria. Legislatures would pass better laws that were in the best interest of everyone. A growing number of schools would connect more students with better teachers. Curricula would be better researched and more students would have a greater opportunity to learn. Roads would be safer in all weather conditions. There would be improved law enforcement to protect the safety of more citizens. Parks would be cleaner and more inviting. Litter and graffiti would be less common. Volunteerism and stewardship would increase significantly.

It is easy to interpret this vision of society as too idealistic and unobtainable. However, skepticism too often becomes fatalism, the justification for inactivity and maintaining the status quo. The enemies of integrity — fear, unwillingness to lose, lack of will, impulsiveness, rationalization, procrastination, fatalism, cynicism, victimism, it's-not-my-job-ism — lurk around every corner and can easily permeate our cultural norms. As Edmund Burke stated, "All that is necessary for evil to triumph is for good people to do nothing" (Britzman, 2000).

There Are Universal Principles, and Consensus Too

It may seem that America's diversity does not lend itself to consensus on teaching basic values. But that conclusion is wrong. A study by the American Federation of Teachers reported that 95 percent of all Americans want public schools to teach honesty and the importance of telling the truth and to respect others regardless of their racial or ethnic background. Ninety-three percent want schools to teach kids to resolve problems without resorting to violence. According to a 1997 survey by the National Association of Secondary School Principals, 78 percent of high school educators believe public education has the responsibility to instill common core values in youth to prepare them to be good citizens.

But before you can ask that of others, especially youth, you have to ask it of yourself.

Living a life of character, and promoting it to others, is not for the faint of heart. All around us swirl messages and examples of selfishness, unrestrained competitiveness and crass materialism.

The place to start is the organizational culture. Children pass through grade levels and eventually leave the school. The young people are not the constant; the organization is. Children must enter into an established culture and feel the desirability of adapting to it. The adults in charge of the organization must change their operational values and behavior first to provide the right culture for children.

Ask yourself some hard questions. How important is good character to your school or organization? Don't look at the "stated values" of written rules and policies. Observe what is actually going on. Is the organization honest with its employees and customers (students)? Is it fair? Does it take responsibility? Is it accountable? Does the organization comply with the law merely to do what it has to, or is there a genuine effort to be ethical? Does the organization have heart? Does it lend a helping hand when it sees a need? Does it respect its employees and customers?

You may believe that your school or youth organization values good character. But remember, you don't have to be sick to get better. There is always room for improvement. The first step is to identify the places, big or small, where the organization falls short. Identify what "is," and begin changing the values by asking why things are that way, and what can be done to make them better. What would we like to see instead? What can we do so the organization reflects the values we want our customers (children) to have?

Psychologists tell us that three things are necessary for change to occur:

- **First, there must be a worthy objective**, one seen as needed and beneficial. With character education, this is a given. Who doesn't want more trustworthiness, respect, responsibility, fairness, caring and good citizenship?

- **Second, the objective must be obtainable**. People must believe they can achieve it. If you were given the charge to make everyone in your city a person of good character, you would probably understand the goal was worthy, yet impossible. However, what about influencing the kids or students under your immediate control? What about the influence you can have on co-workers and friends? As the evidence in this resource shows, that goal is within reach.

- **Third, the objective must be fulfilling**. You have to feel good about it when you reach it. There is intrinsic as well as instrumental value in being a person of good character, having co-workers who have good character, and seeing good character in the children you work with. Each day is easier when you trust those around you and they trust you, when adults and children respect each other, act responsibly, play fair, care for one another and are good citizens of the organization, community, city, country and world.

Taking a Systems View

Become a systems thinker to realistically examine the obstacles you face and the effect you can have.

Your wristwatch is a system, made up of many different parts: cogs, gears, springs, screws, maybe a battery, a case, hands or a digital display, a transparent face. Suppose that the smallest gear in the watch loses just one of its teeth. What will happen to the watch? It could begin running too fast. It could begin running too slow. It could begin running intermittently, starting and stopping at random. Or it might stop running altogether.

Change is constant in the systems perspective. Your watch is always changing; it's moving with time. If it stops changing, then you either get it fixed or you find another watch. In the same way, a systems view reveals that no single moment in the life of any organization tells the whole story about it. Change is occurring at every instant.

Your school or organization is also a system, and it is part of the bigger system of our whole society. Certainly, if your organization is having problems, the place to begin looking is in the organization itself, to repair any problems. However, a systems view shows there may be out-side forces, other systems, affecting your organization. Such other systems include the family, the culture, the economy and the government.

Even small changes in these other systems can affect the school. But the school can change these influential systems too. Consider this: your students are future parents, executives, public servants, entertainers and workers. Change goes in both directions. Schools are not passive victims. So if you want stronger schools tomorrow, schools that are supported rather than undermined by outside systems, then you must help educate for character today.

Notes

1. Carter-Scott, C. (2001). *If high school is a game, here's how to break the rules.* New York, NY: Delacorte Press.

2. Britzman, M.J. (2000). *The lives and legacies of everyday heroes.* Bloomington, IN: Unlimited Publishing.

Putting It All Together: Making Good Decisions

Richard thought it might be fun to scare the younger neighbor boys with a loud noise by secretly shooting his BB gun and ricocheting the BB off a plastic container near where the boys were playing. To his surprise, the BB ricocheted off the plastic and hit one of the boys in the eye. The boy didn't lose his eye, but his vision will probably never be the same.

Clearly, Richard didn't make a good decision. Is that only because of the results? Would it have been a "good decision" if no one got hurt?

Two Principles of Good Decisions. First, we have the power to decide what we do and say, and how we do it or say it. Second, we are morally responsible for the consequences of our choices.

We make decisions all the time. Most are trivial. But some have potentially momentous consequences for the stakeholders — those affected by our decision. Obviously, the greater the potential consequences, the greater the need for careful decision making.

To gauge the seriousness of a decision, ask yourself whether the consequences could:

1. Cause physical harm to you or anyone else.

2. Cause economic loss to you or someone else.

3. Hurt your reputation or your credibility with others.

4. Hurt your relationships with others.

5. Impede achieving any important long-term goals.

Making Good Decisions

Of course, recognizing a serious decision alone isn't enough. We still need to choose correctly. While making good decisions can be difficult and even something of an art, it is true that:

Good decisions are effective. A decision is effective if it achieves what we want, if it advances our purposes. A simple test is: Are we satisfied with the results? A choice that produces unintended and undesirable results is ineffective. For example, if we make a casual remark to make someone feel good, but it makes him feel bad instead, we were ineffective. If we decide to do something we really don't want to do just to please a friend, and the decision ends up getting us in serious trouble, it's ineffective.

Good decisions are ethical. A decision is ethical when it is consistent with the Six Pillars of Character. Ethical decisions generate and sustain trust, and show respect, responsibility, fairness, caring and good citizenship. If we lie to get something we want and we get it, the decision might well be called effective, but it is also unethical.

Ethical decisions require discernment and discipline. Ethical discernment is the ability to see the difference between right and wrong. But *knowing* what is right is not the same as *doing* what is right. That's why ethical decisions also need discipline: the strength of character to do what should be done even when it is costly or uncomfortable. In the vast majority of the ethical problems we face, we know what we should do. The real question is whether we are willing to do the right thing when it costs more than we want to pay.

The Josephson Institute's Ethical Decision-Making Model

This ethical decision-making model — developed by the Josephson Institute of Ethics and advocated by its national **CHARACTER COUNTS!** project — consolidates the wisdom of three historical precepts:

- **The Golden Rule**: Do unto others as you would have them do unto you.

- **Kant's Categorical Imperative:** Ethical obligations are higher truths imposing duties that must be carried out regardless of the consequences and in spite of social conventions and natural inclinations to the contrary.

- **Consequentialism/Utilitarianism:** One should make ethical choices based on their likely consequences. Ethical decisions seek to maximize benefits over burdens, classically producing the greatest good for the greatest number.

This wisdom leads to a very pragmatic, three-step approach:

1. Have I thought about how my decisions are likely to help or hurt others (the "stakeholders")?

2. Am I living up to the Six Pillars of Character by being trustworthy, respectful, responsible, fair, caring and a good citizen, even if I have to give up other things I want?

3. If I cannot find a way to live up to one Six Pillar value without violating another, am I making the choice that I think will be best for society in the long run?

Seven Steps to Making Better Decisions

The key to making effective decisions is to assess choices in terms of how well they achieve our most important goals. To do that we need a structured approach to decision making. The following is a seven-step approach recommended by the Josephson Institute of Ethics (Josephson, 2002):

1. STOP AND THINK

One of the most important steps to better decisions is the oldest advice in the world: think ahead. To do so it's necessary to first stop the momentum of events long enough to permit calm analysis. This may require discipline, but it is a powerful tonic against poor choices.

Avoiding Foolish Behavior. The well-worn formula of counting to 10 when angry and to 100 when very angry is a simple technique designed to prevent foolish and impulsive behavior. But we are just as apt to make foolish decisions when we are under the strain of powerful desires or fatigue, when we are in a hurry or under pressure, and when we are ignorant of important facts.

Just as we teach our children to look both ways before they cross the street, we can and should instill the habit of looking ahead before they make any decision.

Benefits. Stopping to think provides several benefits. It prevents rash decisions. It prepares us for more thoughtful discernment. And it can allow us to mobilize our discipline.

2. CLARIFY GOALS

Before you choose, clarify your short- and long-term aims. Determine which of your many wants and don't-wants affected by the decision are the most important. The big danger is that decisions that fulfill immediate wants and needs can prevent the achievement of our more important life goals. Teen pregnancy is an all-too-typical example of fulfilling immediate desires at the cost of long-term goals.

3. DETERMINE FACTS

Be sure you have adequate information to support an intelligent choice. You can't make good decisions if you don't know the facts.

Gathering Information. To determine the facts, first make clear what you know, then what you need to know. Be prepared to get additional information and to verify assumptions and other uncertainties.

Weigh the Credibility of Sources. Once you begin to be more careful about facts, you often find that there are different versions of them and disagreements about their meaning. In these situations, part of making sound decisions involves making good judgments as to whom and what to believe. Here are some guidelines:

- Consider the reliability and credibility of the people providing the facts.

- Consider the basis of the supposed facts. If the person giving the information says he personally heard or saw something, evaluate that person in terms of honesty, accuracy and memory.

- Remember that assumptions, gossip and hearsay are not the same as facts.

- Consider all perspectives, but be careful to consider whether the source of the information has different values or has a personal interest that could affect perception of the facts.

- Where possible, seek out the opinions of people whose judgment and character are respected, but be careful to distinguish the well-grounded opinions of informed people from casual speculation, conjecture and guesswork.

- Finally, evaluate the information in terms of completeness and reliability to gain a sense of the certainty and fallibility of the decision.

4. DEVELOP OPTIONS

Now that you know what you want to achieve and have made your best judgment as to the relevant facts, make a list of options, a set of actions you can take to accomplish your goals. If it's an especially important decision, consider talking to someone you trust so you can broaden your perspective and think of new choices. If you can think of only one or two choices, you're probably not thinking hard enough.

5. CONSIDER CONSEQUENCES

Filter your choices through each of the Six Pillars of Character (trustworthiness, respect, responsibility, fairness, caring and citizenship). Will the action violate any of the core ethical principles? For instance, does it involve lying or breaking a promise? Is it disrespectful to anyone? Is it irresponsible, unfair or uncaring? Does it involve breaking laws or rules? Eliminate unethical options.

Identify the stakeholders and how the decision is likely to affect them. Consider your choices from the point of view of the major stakeholders. Identify whom the decision will help and hurt.

6. CHOOSE

It's time to make your decision. If the choice is not immediately clear, consider the following strategies:

Talk to people whose judgment you respect. Seek out friends and mentors, but remember, once you've gathered opinions and advice, the responsibility is still yours.

What would the most ethical person you know do? Think of the person you know or know of (in real life or fiction) who has the strongest character and best ethical judgment. Then ask: what would that person do in your situation? Think of that person as your decision-making role model and try to behave the way he or she would. Many Christians wear a small bracelet with the letters WWJD standing for the question "What would Jesus do?" Whether you are Christian or not, the idea of referencing a role model can be a useful one. You could translate the question into: "What would God want me to do?" "What would Buddha or Mother Teresa do?" "What would Gandhi do?" "What would the most virtuous person in the world do?"

What would you do if you were sure everyone would know? If everyone found out about your decision, would you be proud and comfortable? Choices that only look good if no one knows are always bad choices. Good choices make us worthy of admiration and build good reputations. It's been said that character is revealed by how you behave when you think no one is looking and is strengthened when you act as if everyone is looking.

Apply the Golden Rule. Do unto others as you would have them do unto you. The Golden Rule is one of the oldest and best guides to ethical decision making. If you treat people the way you want to be treated, you are likely to live up to the Six Pillars of Character. You don't want to be lied to or have promises broken, so you should be honest and keep your promises to others. You want others to treat you with respect, so you should treat others respectfully.

7. MONITOR AND MODIFY

Corrective Course Changes Are OK. Since most hard decisions use imperfect information and "best effort" predictions, some will inevitably be wrong. Ethical decision makers monitor the effects of their choices. If they are not producing the intended results or are causing additional unintended and undesirable results, then reassess the situation and make new decisions.

The Josephson Institute's Seven-Step model is very good — if you have the time! But what about when the pressure is on and you have to make a decision at once? Let's be honest: We make most of our ethical choices in the heat of the moment. What do we do then?

"First, Do No Harm." When we make ethical decisions, we first should strive to avoid doing harm, and then try to produce good, as much as possible, for everyone involved.

Good Decisions Are Rational, Not Rationalizations

Rational decisions are the result of a careful reasoning process, evaluating the effectiveness and ethics of options. Rationalizations arise to justify choices the decision maker wants to make or has already made. For example, should we "pad" (lie on) our resume when applying for a job? A rational decision maker would examine the ethics and possible consequences of that option. A rationalizer would say, "Other people do it, and if I want to get this job, I have to do the same to be able to compete with them."

Here are other common rationalizations:

- **If It's Legal and Permissible, It's Proper.** This substitutes rules and legal requirements (which establish only minimal standards of behavior) for personal moral judgment. The law hardly embraces the full range of ethical obligations, especially for individuals involved in upholding the public trust. Ethical people often choose to do less than the maximally allowable, and more than the minimally acceptable.

- **It's Just Part of the Job.** Conscientious people who want to do their jobs well often fail to adequately consider the morality of their professional behavior. They tend to compartmentalize ethics into two domains: private and occupational. Fundamentally decent people thereby feel justified doing things at work that they know to be wrong in other contexts. They forget that everyone's first job is to be a good person.

- **It's All for a Good Cause.** People are especially vulnerable to rationalizations when they seek to advance a noble aim. "It's all for a good cause" is a seductive rationale that loosens interpretations of deception, concealment, conflicts of interest, favoritism and violations of established rules and procedures.

- **I Was Just Doing It for You.** This is a primary justification for committing "little white lies" or withholding important information in personal or professional relationships, such as performance reviews. This rationalization pits the values of honesty and respect against the value of caring. An individual deserves the truth because he has a moral right to make decisions about his own life based on accurate information. This rationalization overestimates other people's desire to be "protected" from the truth, when in fact most people would rather know unpleasant information than believe soothing falsehoods. Consider the perspective of people lied to: If they discovered the lie, would they thank us for being thoughtful or would they feel betrayed, patronized or manipulated?

- **I'm Just Fighting Fire With Fire.** This is the false assumption that promise-breaking, lying and other kinds of misconduct are justified if they are routinely engaged in by those with whom you are dealing. Remember: when we fight fire with fire, we end up with the ashes of our own integrity.

- **It Doesn't Hurt Anyone.** Used to excuse misconduct, this rationalization falsely holds that one can violate ethical principles so long as there is no clear and immediate harm to others. It treats ethical obligations simply as factors to be considered in decision making, rather than as ground rules. Problem areas: asking for or giving special favors to family, friends or public officials; disclosing nonpublic information to benefit others; using one's position for personal advantage.

- **Everyone's Doing It.** This is a false, "safety in numbers" rationale fed by the tendency to uncritically treat cultural, organizational or occupational behaviors as if they were ethical norms, just because they are commonplace.

- **It's OK As Long As I Don't Gain Personally.** This justifies improper conduct done for others or for institutional purposes on the false assumption that personal gain is the only test of impropriety. A related but narrower view is that only behavior resulting in improper financial gain warrants ethical criticism.

- **I've Got It Coming.** People who feel they are overworked or underpaid rationalize that minor "perks" — such as acceptance of favors, discounts or gratuities — are nothing more than fair compensation for services rendered. This is also used as an excuse to abuse sick time, insurance claims, overtime, personal phone calls and personal use of office supplies.

- **I Can Still Be Objective.** By definition, if we've lost our objectivity, we can't see that we've lost our objectivity! It also underestimates the subtle ways in which gratitude, friendship and the anticipation of future favors affect judgment. Does the person providing us with the benefit believe that it will in no way affect our judgment? Would the person still provide the benefit if we were in no position to help?

Notes

1. Josephson, M. (2002). *Making ethical decisions.* Los Angeles, CA: Josephson Institute of Ethics.

Conclusion:
Leaving a Legacy of Change

Teachers, as Henry Adams said, affect all eternity. But some have more impact than others, and a true education leader will change a culture and leave a legacy in both the institution and in all the young people who go forth from it into the world. One person can really make a difference, and the statement is no less true for being often repeated.

You face myriad challenges every day that test the strength of your character. Your efforts are most likely fueled by a deep need to establish an environment for each student to maximize his or her potential, making our world a better place. Each day is an opportunity for students to build stronger character through exposure to role models who demonstrate the Six Pillars of Character. Our youth comprise 27 percent of our population and 100 percent of the future.

The following poem — written by Michael Josephson, founder and president of **CHARACTER COUNTS!** — contains key insights about the effort to lead an ethical life, the true legacy of an education leader:

The older I get the less I know, but I know some things:

I know that I'm a work in progress and that there will always be a gap between who I am and who I want to be.

I know that I don't have to be sick to get better and that every day brings opportunities to improve my life and my character.

I know that it's easier to talk about integrity than to live it and that the true test is my willingness to do the right thing even when it costs more than I want to pay.

I know that character is more important than competence.

I know that it takes years to build up trust and only seconds to destroy it.

I know that I often judge myself by my best intentions and most noble acts, but that I'll be judged by my last worst act.

I know that I can't control what will happen to me but that I have a lot to say about what happens in me.

I know that pain is inevitable, but suffering is optional.

I know that attitudes, both good and bad, are contagious.

I know that winning is more than coming in first and that there's no real victory without honor.

I know that it takes a conscientious effort to be kind, but that kindness changes lives.

I know that neither gratitude nor forgiveness comes naturally; both often require acts of will.

I know that real success is being significant.

I know that happiness is deeper and more enduring than either pleasure or fun and that I'm generally as happy as I'm willing to be.

I know that the surest road to happiness is good relationships, and that the best way to have good relationships is to be a good person.

Character education lends strength and hope to every youngster. To be worthy, you don't have to be popular, brilliant, athletic, wealthy or attractive. You must simply be dedicated to making good decisions based on principle rather than expediency, and be willing to improve your behavior. We can all live lives of significance, and greater happiness, if we just do that.

The national office of **CHARACTER COUNTS!** is happy to help you. Call **(800) 711-2670** or visit its website at **www.charactercounts.org** to learn more about getting involved. We look forward to working with you, and perhaps meeting you at an upcoming Character Development Seminar.

Other titles to inspire and enrich your character-building efforts

More resources from the Josephson Institute of Ethics

(8.5" x 11", softcover, 72 pages)
Item #50-4010
$14.95

Parenting: The Most Important Job of Your Life

In partnership with the National PTA, **CHARACTER COUNTS!** has created this state-of-the-art tool for parents and guardians.

A parent's job is to prepare children for life, and there is no better way than to consciously help them develop strong character. But where are the instructions? How do we train children to have the desire and strength to do what's right and avoid what's wrong?

The guide offers parents practical advice and suggests creative activities for kids in six age groups: 0-3, 4-6, 6-9, 9-11, 11-13 and 13-18.

Commentaries by Michael Josephson

Every day, listeners around the world tune in to hear Michael Josephson's take on the issues that define our days and lives. From business and world affairs to sports and parenting, Mr. Josephson offers the unique perspective of one of the country's best-known ethicists and most innovative teachers. Now his favorite commentaries — featuring the humor, compassion and tough talk he is renowned for — are available in these hardcover gift volumes and in a two-CD set.

(Books are 5" x 7", hardcover with dust jacket)

You Don't Have to Be Sick to Get Better!	**Item #50-5000**	**$20.00**
The Best Is Yet to Come	**Item #50-5010**	**$20.00**
Both books	**Item #50-5020sp**	**$35.00**
Making Your Character Count double CD	**Item #05-1190**	**$20.00**

Making Ethical Decisions

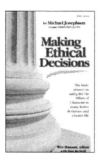

Moral questions can be knotty. This comprehensive primer examines the hows and whys of making choices that withstand ethical scrutiny. With realistic examples and a step-by-step decision-making model, this easy-to-read booklet is ideal for the individual reader — or as a training guide for any organization that wishes to help its employees find the way through difficult issues to successful choices.

(5.5" x 8.5", softcover, 33 pages)
Item #50-0450
$7.95

Order books on this page by calling (800) 711-2670 or online at
www.charactercounts.org